3000 Years of Art and Life in Mexico

3000 Years
of Art and Life in Mexico

AS SEEN IN

The National Museum of Anthropology, Mexico City

★

BY IGNACIO BERNAL,

WITH ROMÁN PIÑA-CHÁN

AND FERNANDO CÁMARA-BARBACHANO

PHOTOGRAPHS BY IRMGARD GROTH

★

HARRY N. ABRAMS, INC. *Publishers* NEW YORK

Translated from the Spanish by Carolyn B. Czitrom

Library of Congress Catalog Card Number: 68–8978
Harry N. Abrams, Incorporated, New York
Printed and bound in Great Britain

Contents

1 The Museum's large central patio, looking towards the Vestibule from outside the Mexica Hall

2 View from the Vestibule across the central patio

The Origins, Aims, and Achievements of the Museum

The study of anthropology – although not under this name – has been pursued in Mexico for many centuries. Very soon after the Spanish Conquest friars, missionaries, conquerors, and descendants of the indigenous nobility who had received a European-type education began to record their experiences, write grammars and vocabularies for the various languages spoken in Mesoamerica, as well as the history of their ancestors. Towards the middle of the sixteenth century enterprising men began to assemble what they could of the old myths and legends, the ancient customs and traditions, building up an exceptionally rich corpus of documents of many kinds. The most remarkable of these scholars – Fray Bernardino de Sahagún (c. 1499–1590) by assiduously tapping a wide variety of local sources assembled so much material that he was able to write a wide-ranging treatise on the ethnology of the region, which has in my opinion no equal.

The purpose of this vast labour of investigation and salvage was not solely academic. For the Spaniards it arose from the need to understand the vanquished peoples on whom the budding colony was founded; for the indigenes it was a matter of recalling past glories and sometimes of obtaining advantages and favours from the new political power. But by the beginning of the seventeenth century this great movement came to an end.

By contrast, the material remains of the ancient cultures were destroyed without scruple. The greed of the conquerors for gold resulted in the melting down of jewels; their urge to extirpate the pagan religion and spread Christianity in its stead caused the statues of the gods to be shattered and majestic temples to be demolished. Some towns were abandoned but on the sites of most of the native cities arose new, European-style houses. Owing to ignorance and indifference these new cities covered over what remained of the ancient monuments, and these sank into an obscurity from which modern archaeology has only recently begun to free them.

Although during the seventeenth and the first half of the eighteenth century there were a few inquiring minds who took an interest in discovering objects and documents and investigating the already remote past, it was not until the end of the Vice-regal period that a distinguished group of Mexicans – the first Mexicans – began to accord these documents and relatively few surviving objects their due importance, realizing that through them the country's forgotten history could be reconstructed.

Clavijero, Alzate, Márquez, and others were dedicated to this task, inspired by the new ideas of the Enlightenment, a movement which even prompted Charles III of Spain to send an archaeological mission to Mexico. The chance discovery in 1790 of three immense monoliths – the Sun Stone, the statue of Coatlicue, and the monument to the victories of Tizoc – now housed in the Museum, served to sound the alert. The first Mexican archaeologist, Antonio de Leon y Gama, published these carvings, and unlike the procedure hitherto adopted, instead of being destroyed they were preserved – the Sun Stone beside the Cathedral, Coatlicue and the Tizoc monument in the University. This was really the genesis of the Museum, though it was not to be legally established until 1825 on behest of the historian Lucas Alamán. Gradually, although with no definite plan or authentic data as to provenance, more and more pieces were accumulated in a large hall which the University assigned to them. However haphazard the first assortment may have appeared, it is to this initial intent that we owe the salvage of many unique objects. Finally on 5 December 1865 Maximilian signed an agreement whereby an old palace on Moneda Street was assigned to the new National Museum.

At that time it was a general museum containing not only prehispanic material but also mementoes of Mexican history and natural science collections. It was not until 1940 that – everything else being removed – the Museum was dedicated exclusively to anthropological material. The newly aroused interest in the subject, the enormous growth of the collection mainly as a result of the many explorations carried out in the preceding 30 years, and the considerable advances made in the science, meant that the rambling building soon became inadequate for its purpose. However, these were not the only reasons for a change.

In recent years Mexico has progressed in a remarkable way; besides making great strides on the material plane, it has come to realize what it means to be the heir of two civilizations and to belong to a culture that is a combination of both; just as it is impossible to deny either a father or a mother, so the country must fulfil its destiny by a proud affirmation of this hybrid civilization. It was with this in mind that President Lopez Mateos decided to construct a magnificent palace for housing the indigenous cultures, and at the same time display the Viceregal collections in a worthy manner within an appropriate frame.

The Museum's dual aim has been to do full justice to the collections while making every endeavour to ensure that the visitor shall derive the maximum benefit from the time he spends in the halls. This is not an art museum but a museum of history. The fact that many of the objects are masterpieces of ancient art can be regarded as a happy bonus over and above the main objective, namely, to get to know and understand to the best of our ability the significance of indigenous Mexico and to relate it to the united country that we all want to create.

In order to achieve these ends in a scientifically valid form the collection had to be presented in clear and logical order, not as miscellaneous items but as vestiges of a civilization. That is why, after progressing through an initiatory hall that gives the visitor a general idea of the meaning and scope of anthropology, he passes on to an introductory hall on Mesoamerica where the various cultures are linked in such a way as to show that together they form a single civilization. Styles co-ordinated by regions or by periods as presented in the other halls tend to suggest that each one is isolated, since it is precisely these differences which characterize them; but they are intelligible only if it is understood that all form part of a common world and that the basic similarities are much more important than regional variations.

The other halls of the north wing trace the sequence of cultures in the central region of Mexico from their most remote origins, through the great Preclassic, Teotihuacán, and Toltec stages, down to the Aztec world. The south wing is devoted to the regional cultures of Oaxaca, Veracruz, the Maya region, North and West Mexico, again arranged in chronological order. Thus the visitor can travel not only through the whole country but also through time, with each exhibit evoking a certain period.

But the natural limitations of a museum must be remembered. It can never be a substitute for books, and the physical presence of objects from the past will only present a true picture of history if they are accompanied by related reading.

The Museum – located in Chapultepec Park facing the Paseo de la Reforma – occupies an area of some 125,000 square metres. Such a site, besides offering many practical and aesthetic advantages, is particularly appropriate since Chapultepec has countless historical associations, being among other things the place in the Valley where the Aztecs first chose to settle.

The building has 44,000 square metres under cover and 35,700 square metres of open spaces, including the central patio and large plaza forming the entrance, and the sunken patios surrounding it. Spacious lawns separate the Museum from the streets and there is ample space for the parking of cars. The wooded park forms a handsome setting not only for the display halls but also for the general offices, the Library, and the School of Anthropology.

Crossing the large entrance plaza one enters a central vestibule of vast proportions. In the centre of this is a raised area with beneath it the Orientation Room containing a small amphi-theatre where the visitor is treated to a pageant preparing him for his visit to the Museum. This takes the form of a recorded commentary illustrated by a succession of models and photographs, all automatically operated.

To the right of the vestibule is a large hall devoted to temporary exhibits, and beyond this an auditorium for nearly four hundred people. Various offices and storerooms occupy the left side of the vestibule. Above is the Library which has a large, pleasantly appointed reading room and all the appropriate accessories such as the Historic Archives, Department of Codices, microfilm projectors, and Archives for this section – with some twelve million documents – and the Library storage with room for nearly half a million books.

On a mezzanine floor below the Museum and to the right are ample storerooms for the Archaeology, Ethnography, and Physical Anthropology sections, which contain not only its vast reserve collections but also space for future acquisitions. Adjacent to these are the technical offices and laboratories. On the left are the rooms of the scholastic services where children are prepared for their visit to the museum, and a sunken patio through which one reaches a side staircase leading up to the central patio.

From the central vestibule through an entrance in a glass wall one gains access to the large patio round which are ranged the display halls. The first part of the patio is covered by a graceful roof measuring 82 by 84 metres with only one central support, and adorned with sculptured copper; from above falls a circle of water that forms an inverse fountain.

The great ornamental patio beyond, with a rectangular pool in the centre, allows the visitor access to the various halls of the Museum without compelling him to follow any particular route; like the displays set in gardens adjoining some of the halls, it serves to dispel the museum atmosphere and allows him an occasional respite.

Ignacio Bernal

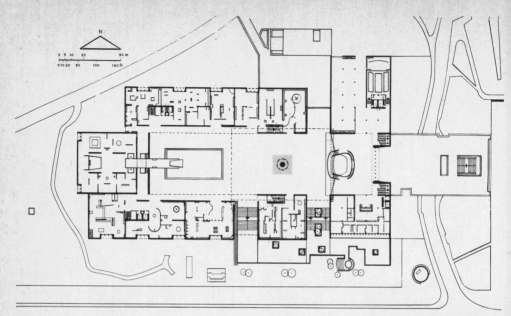

(*Above left*) Ground-floor plan of Museum

(*Above right*) First-floor plan of Museum

3 View of main entrance to the Museum

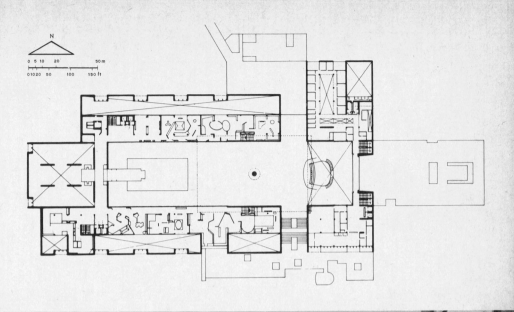

Introduction to Anthropology

The diverse indigenous cultures of Mexico, both those which flourished in prehistoric times and those which have persisted until the present day, present anthropology with a vast field for study while providing museums with rich and valuable materials for display. At the same time they constitute a major part of the history and the cultural inheritance of the country, the knowledge, dissemination, and conservation of which constantly gain in importance.

Keeping this in mind, those who planned the new National Museum of Anthropology decided to include an initiatory hall that would justify the Museum's name and at the same time present a universal framework into which the Mexican cultures could be fitted in space and in time, as well as allowing visitors to compare their cultural contributions with those of other peoples.

The Introductory Hall to Anthropology was thus established to explain what this science is, the various branches it covers, its aims and methods of work, and what has been achieved in its study of man. There are four interrelated sections corresponding to the four basic branches of the subject: physical anthropology, archaeology, linguistics, and ethnography.

The section on physical anthropology begins with the question of man's origin and his biological evolution. The subject is illustrated with drawings, chronological charts, and fossil reproductions, emphasis being placed on the dynamic process of evolution – through genetic and morphological change – and on the position occupied by man in the animal kingdom, his antiquity, and his relation to other primates.

Special displays show advances made in the study of physical anthropology, such as the determining of age and sex in deceased or living individuals, for demographic purposes; craniology, or classification of individuals and groups into dolichocephalic, mesocephalic, and brachycephalic types; dental mutilations and cranial deformation; trepanation; growth and stature of individuals, as well as demographic increase in populations, as these are linked to dietetic and nutritional problems, and biotypology, which shows the relation between corporal structure and the behaviour of human beings.

Finally, this section illustrates work done in connection with certain hereditary factors such as steatopygia, eye colour, and the mongolian spot, as well as on the classification of human beings by blood groups. The section as a whole stresses the basic aim of physical anthropology, which is to study biological aspects of human populations, past and present, and the application of such knowledge to medicine and public health.

The relation between man and his culture is introduced in the section assigned to archaeology, which focuses on vanished indigenous cultures. Here the subject is broached by explaining the purpose of stratigraphy, basic to archaeology since stratigraphic layers hold remains that are a key to man's activities and enable us to determine what the inhabitants of any one place were like and how they lived in different periods.

The field work and studies that the archaeologist must carry out are shown next, among which we find the reconnaissance of archaeological areas, excavation of test pits and trenches, the exploration of burial and ritual offerings, cleaning and reconstruction of buildings, protection of perishable materials or mural paintings, and many others. All this serves to establish typologies for ceramics and artifacts, chronologies, the nature of funerary practices, and artistic manifestations; in short, to interpret and integrate the history of a culture.

In this way archaeologists have been able to reconstruct the cultural development of man from the most remote times until the advent of civilization. We are shown salient features of the main prehistoric periods: the Lower Palaeolithic, in which man lived from hunting and gathering and had the use of fire; the Middle Palaeolithic, when artifacts became more specialized; and the Upper Palaeolithic, during which man improved his tools – adding the ability to carve stone, shell, and ivory – and the origins of art appear in cave paintings. We then progress to the Mesolithic Age, when man first experiments with the cultivation of certain plants, and small villages appear; and the Neolithic period in which agriculture is developed, pottery begins, animals are domesticated and herding is practised. All these developments are antecedent to future civilization.

Objects from various parts of the world are used to illustrate the achievements made by different ancient civilizations – among them those of Mesopotamia, the Indus Valley, Egypt, and Peru – and comparisons are made with Mesoamerica so that its achievements may be seen in a universal context. By means of displays, dioramas, drawings, and photographs this section conveys an idea of the slow cultural development of man and the progress he has achieved, which is the aim of archaeology.

In the central part of the hall is a section on linguistics, the branch of anthropology that investigates the origin and development of human language, how languages change and may disappear, how vanished languages can be reconstructed, how they are classified, and how this study contributes to a better understanding of man's history. These various aspects are illustrated with archaeological and ethnographic materials, maps, and audiovisual equipment. Mention is also made of other means of communication, namely by gesture, mimicry, and signalling with banners, fans, horns, and conch shells. Also included is writing, the principal visual means of communication among men by which ideas and cultural advances are disseminated.

The fourth section of this hall is devoted to social ethnology, which studies present-day man and his society by investigating communities, consulting bibliographies, selecting themes and informants, preparing questionnaires, and applying modern techniques to social research. The knowledge thus gained is classified and further elaborated with statistics, graphs, maps, and charts to facilitate the work.

In this way the ethnologist is able to trace the boundaries of natural and ethnic areas and define the characteristics of their economy, technology, social and family organization, systems of social control, philosophy, and art – in short, to arrive at the basic outline of a particular culture. He then goes on to compare a particular social institution with those found in other parts of the world, relates their historical antecedents to general history, determines the level of development attained by the society under review, and tries to establish social and cultural laws valid for all mankind.

By way of illustrating the economic and technological aspects of various types of cultures, the material evidence provided by characteristic groups is displayed: the Eskimos as an example of hunters and gatherers; the Sakai, who are principally gatherers; the Haidas, with a system of specialized fishing; and the Bosquimanos, who thanks to their ingenuity survive in an inhospitable environment; the Hopis, with an inferior level of agriculture, and the Lapps, who live from their herds of reindeer. All this demonstrates that man has adequate means for survival, and that his economy and technology develop in accordance with his environment.

Aspects of religion and magic are also treated – illustrated by means of objects from various cultures – as well as science, art, and social organization. Numerous artifacts of the Eskimos are used to show the manner in which the ethnologist interprets a particular culture.

In this hall the visitor is finally shown present-day applications of anthropology, embracing the reconstruction of archaeological sites, studies of ancient history, programmes of health and public assistance, studies of child development, the planning of modern communities, bilingual primers for education work, and so on. By way of conclusion the message is conveyed – again illustrated with material from various cultures – that all peoples have the same capacity for resolving their needs, and only vary as to resources and procedures. It is this that defines a particular culture, although culture itself is the patrimony of all mankind, to which all peoples at all times have contributed.

Regions and archaeological sites of Mesoamerica

Chronological Table

RELATIVE DATING		
HORIZONS	POSTCLASSIC	
PERIODS	LATE / EARLY	TR

Time scale (top to bottom): 1500, 1400, 1300, 1200, 1100, 1000, 900, 800, 700, 600, 500, 400, 300, 200, 100, 0, 100, 200, 300, 400, 500, 600, 700, 800, 900, 1000, 1100, 1200, 1300, 1400, 1500, 1600

HORIZONS: POSTCLASSIC — CLASSIC — FORMATIVE OR PRECLASSIC

PERIODS: LATE · EARLY · TR · LATE · EARLY · PROTOCLASSIC · UPPER · MIDDLE · LOWER

CENTRAL HIGHLANDS
MEXICA · TOLTECS · TEOTI HUACAN IV · III · II · I · TLATILCO II · TLATILCO I · COPILCO · CUICUILCO

GULF COAST
CEMPOALA · TOTONACS · EL TAJIN I-8 · REMOJADAS III · OLMECS LA VENTA II · OLMECS LA VENTA I

OAXACA
HUASTECS · PANUCO III · PANUCO II · PANUCO I · AGUILAR · PONCE · PAVON · ZAPOTECS V · IV · TR IIIB · TR IIIA · II · I (TR) · MIXTECS GENEALOGIES · MONTE ALBAN I

MAYA
MAYA · CHENES PUUC · TEPEU · TZAKOL · MATZANEL · CHICANEL · MAMON

WESTERN MEXICO
TARASCANS · DELICIAS · CHUMBICUARO · JIQUILPAN · APATZINGAN · CHUPICUARO · EL OPENO · GUASAVE · AZTATLAN COMPLEX · CHAMETLA I-II

Mesoamerica

A general frame of reference for the indigenous culture of Mexico having been established in the initiatory hall it was decided to supplement this with another introductory hall which would coordinate the various elements or cultural traits common to the peoples of Mesoamerica, its chronology, and the main features of its topography. This was considered necessary not only because various prehispanic cultures developed in this region, but also to avoid the need for repeating explanations in each of the halls devoted to specific cultures.

The area of advanced culture called Mesoamerica includes a large part of the Mexican Republic; its northern border is formed by the Soto La Marina River in the State of Tamaulipas and the Sinaloa River, and it extends southward to the Gulf of Nicoya in Costa Rica and the Motagua River in Honduras.

Within this large territory the Olmecs, Teotihuacanos, Toltecs, Aztecs, Huastecs, Totonacs, Tarascans, Zapotecs, Mixtecs, Maya, and other groups developed and flourished, and varying numbers of their descendants still live there today. Their cultures can be recognized by works of art in which the regional styles or traditions of each period are clearly distinguishable.

A map in colour defines the territory of Mesoamerica and shows its cultural zones with their most characteristic crafts. For example, for West Mexico there are polychrome pottery from Sinaloa; hollow figurines from Colima and Nayarit; the *yácatas* and pipes from Michoacán; stone carving from Mezcala, Guerrero, and figurines and pottery from Chupícuaro, Guanajuato. The Gulf Coast depicts sculptures and pottery of the Huastecs; *hachas*, palmate stones, yokes, and smiling figures from central Veracruz; and the colossal Olmec heads and jade figures from southern Veracruz and northern Tabasco.

Depicted too are Teotihuacán mural paintings and vases with lids; the enormous statues or atlantes of the Toltecs in Tula, Hidalgo, and the twin temples and sculptures of the Aztecs, which as a group distinguish the region of the Central Highlands. The same applies to the clay urns of the Zapotecs and the polychrome pottery, metallurgy, and codices of the Mixtecs, who occupied the Oaxaca region. Stelae, buildings, pottery, and modelling in stucco are characteristic of the Maya, who occupied Palenque, Bonampak, Yaxchilán, Chichen Itzá, Tulúm, and many other sites.

All these cultures evolved in geographic regions that show many elements in common, and their chronological periods ran more or less parallel. A specially designed device presents a clear picture of the progress of the various cultures, and serves as a chronological-cultural frame of reference. We are shown the Preclassic horizon and its period of development (1700–200 BC), during which the Mesoamerican groups were basically agricultural, produced an advanced pottery, buried their dead, initiated the construction of temple bases and the worship of deities, as a priestly caste evolved. All this led to the birth of civilization during the Classic horizon (200 BC–AD 800), a period characterized by large ceremonial centres, the development of crafts and trades, learning, a complex religion, intensive agriculture, and many other cultural achievements.

Finally, the same chart shows how, in the Postclassic horizon (AD 800–1521), the theocratic societies turn militaristic, conquer other peoples and impose tribute; fortified cities appear, metallurgy is introduced, as well as new irrigation techniques in agriculture, and new crafts evolve. The codices appear as the first historic written sources, their development later being cut short by the Spanish Conquest.

Displays of archaeological objects, together with drawings, photographs, models, etc., serve to illustrate various cultural traits which were common to all the prehispanic peoples. In reference to agriculture, it is seen that various farming systems were used such as planting in marshes or in the silt deposited after floods on the banks of rivers and lake shores, *milpas* or corn fields which were sown on valley floors and the flanks of surrounding hills; terracing; artificial irrigation by means of canals, and the *chinampas* or 'floating' garden beds built into the lakes. By such methods these peoples cultivated corn, squash, beans, chilli, amaranth, sweet potato, cacao, *chia* (flax seed), avocado, tobacco, cotton, and many other utilitarian and medicinal plants which after the Spanish Conquest came into almost universal use.

In hunting and fishing the Mesoamerican groups used the *atlatl* or spear-thrower, the javelin, bow and arrow, blowpipe, slings, traps, harpoons, fish-hooks, fish spear, canoes, nets, and even poisons to render the fish insensible. These things enabled them to catch deer, wild turkeys, wild boar, ducks, armadillos, rabbits, turtles, white fish, manatees, jaguars, quetzals (macaws), and many other species of animals for use both as food and as material for applying to handicrafts.

Ills. 5, 10   To distinguish one group from another or to denote rank – and even to achieve their ideal of beauty – the Mesoamerican peoples practised cranial deformation, dental mutilation, and tattooing or scarification; they painted their bodies and faces, dyed their hair and teeth, and shaved their heads and beards. The nasal septum, lower lip, and ear lobes were perforated in order to insert various kinds of plugs. They wore bead necklaces, bracelets, rings, pectorals, bells, ankle bracelets, mirrors, and other ornaments, made of many different materials.

Ill. 4   The various groups wore simple articles of clothing, the material and decoration used depending on social status and occupation. Loin-cloths, short skirts, tunics, *huipiles* and *quechquemitls* (a triangular over-blouse), sashes, long cloaks, sandals, hats, fans, shields, conical hats, and staffs of office were among the items used either by the élite or by commoners.

At first the rural or agricultural communities comprised individuals or groups who were governed by a caste of shamans or magicians, but later a theocratic type of society developed with ceremonial centres in which the highest caste or estate was composed of priests, warriors, nobles, merchants, and minor functionaries. Next came an intermediate class made up of craftsmen, artists, aides of priests, and other persons of lower rank; and on the lowest level were the common people. This type of organization – based on a social hierarchy and clearly defined activities – lasted until the Spanish Conquest, although by then it was militaristic rather than theocratic.

Pottery, which was produced by all the Mesoamerican cultures but each one in a style of its own, is given prominence in this hall. Outstanding are the beautiful zoomorphic forms from Tlatilco, polychrome vessels of Chupícuaro, bowls and fresco-decorated vases from Teotihuacán, urns with representations of gods of the Zapotecs, polychrome vases and plates made by the Maya, as well as polychrome vessels of the Mixtecs that are painted with motifs like those of the pictorial books.

The use of metals – including gold- and silversmiths' work – is also shown; in this it was mainly the Mixtecs and Tarascans who excelled. They worked gold, silver, copper, *tumbaga* – an alloy of gold, silver, and copper – as well as an alloy of tin and copper. With these metals and using techniques of cold hammering, *cire-perdue* (lost-wax) casting, gilding, filigree work, soldering, and repoussé, they made laminated bracelets, disks with reliefs, pectorals, rings, bells, tweezers, needles, handles for fans, and many other items.

Work in wood, stone, and shell is also on view; combs, awls, needles, handles for fans, staffs of office, benches, canoes, and musical instruments were all produced from these materials. As carvers of stone and engravers of precious gems the Olmecs of Central Veracruz, the Maya, and the Aztecs were outstanding. Such skills are evidenced by colossal heads and monolithic altars, yokes and palmate stones, stelae and tablets with hieroglyphic inscriptions, as well as imposing statues of gods.

In the Mesoamerican Hall one section is devoted to burials; here diverse methods adopted by the prehispanic peoples for disposing of their dead are illustrated. There is also a section concerned with religion, in which some of the principal deities are indicated. This aspect of Mesoamerican culture is evoked by Raul Anguiano in a mural painting which depicts Mictlante-cuhtli, god of death; Tepeyolotli, god of the inner recesses of the earth; Chicomecoatl and Coatlicue, who together rule the Underworld; also Tezcatlipoca, Yum Kaax, Xipe, and Quetzalcoatl, who were gods related to the earth; and Tlaloc, Ehecatl, Tonatiuh, Huehueteotl, and Ix Tab, the celestial gods. The figures portrayed are taken from the codices and archaeological remains of various groups.

Another important facet of Mesoamerican culture which is here taken into account concerns the intellectual achievements of the prehispanic peoples; these include hieroglyphic writing and numeration, the invention of zero, the vigesimal system, the making of codices and maps, astronomical observations regarding Venus and the sun, the establishment of a calendar of 365 days and the precise length of lunar cycles, as well as knowledge of geography, history, and medicinal herbs, literature and poetry, and architecture.

Finally, visitors to the Museum can see the evolution of the pyramidal temple base, which was the principal element of the ceremonial centres and served to define architectural style; there is a series of models showing successively the simple platforms of the Cerro del Tepalcate; then the superposing of platforms giving rise to stepped bases like that of Cuicuilco; next, the pyramidal base known as the Pyramid of the Sun at Teotihuacán; and finally, the bases supporting twin temples like those of Tenochtitlán. Together they elucidate the development of religious architecture in the Central Highlands.

For purposes of comparison the pyramidal bases of Tikal, Palenque, and Chichen Itzá – cities that flourished in the Maya region – are also shown. A model of Teotihuacán is displayed to give an idea of prehispanic ceremonial centres. Closely associated with architecture is mural painting, used for embellishing buildings, terraces, statues, codices, and pottery; these mostly take the form of fragments of frescoes and painted pottery vessels, from various Mesoamerican cultures.

4 Polychrome figure wearing hat, perhaps a dancer. Clay. Central Vera-cruz. Height: 15 cm. Classic

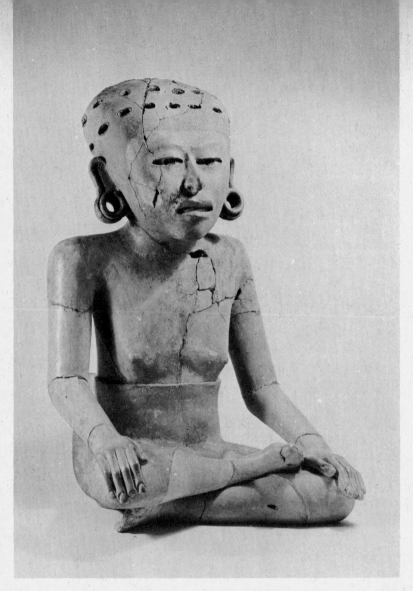

5 Seated woman with deformed and shaven head. Clay. Central Veracruz. Height: 45 cm. Classic

6 *(right)* Relief showing celestial deity holding the umbilical cord of a skeletal individual, possibly the god of death. Stone. Izapa, Chiapas. Height: 1.52 m. Protoclassic

The Origins

Let there be light!
Let the dawn rise over heavens and earth!
There can be no glory, no splendour
Until the human being exists,
The fully developed man.

Popol Vuh

As the name indicates, this hall shows the populating of Mexico, provides archaeological evidence for prehistoric periods of development, analyses their cultural components, and makes comparison with similar groups in North America. The settling of this continent was the result of various migrations coming from Asia, the earliest of which occurred at least 25,000 years before our era, as the opening exhibits of the hall show. The majority of these people came through the Bering Strait, although in more recent times others may have crossed the Pacific Ocean; the latter, however, are of minor importance compared with those from the north of Asia.

The first migrations of any consequence took place during the last glaciation – known as the Wisconsin – which affected the northern part of the American continent. A sort of ice bridge was formed between Asia and America enabling man to enter the new continent, and these people subsequently spread in successive waves over all of North America – including Mexico – as well as Central and South America.

The newcomers depended for their subsistence on hunting, fishing, and food-gathering. They had the use of fire, and hunted large Pleistocene animals that furnished them with meat, bone, and skins; these pelts were used to protect their bodies from the cold and as coverings for tents or lean-tos. Their stone implements were similar to those of the Upper Palaeolithic of the Old World, consisting of choppers, scrapers, and elementary forms of grindstones.

Among the first settlers, the long or dolichocephalic skull predominated, but people with brachycephalic or wide skulls arrived later. In time these gave rise to intermediate types. This is indicated on a distribution map displayed in the hall. It is then shown how this information, considered in conjunction with associated tools that reveal the cultural level, enables us to identify the most ancient inhabitants of any locality.

The first settlers in Mexico had a low level of material culture; an industry of stone flakes and pebbles together with certain projectile points which were later refined are evidence of successive modes of primitive subsistence. These progressive stages and their principal artifacts are tabulated as a chronological sequence which – although its nomenclature is not accepted by all investigators – is perhaps appropriate for Mexico.

This chronological-cultural sequence begins with the Archaeolithic period (25,000–12,000 B C) and covers a primitive stage of food-gatherers using simple tools shaped from rocks or pebbles. The ensuing Lower Cenolithic (12,000–7000 B C) corresponds to the first hunters of Pleistocene fauna when the first projectile points appeared. Next comes the Upper Cenolithic (7000–5000 B C) marking the extinction of the large animals and the transition of man to a basically food-gathering existence. Finally, we have the Protoneolithic (5000–2500 B C) in which agriculture is discovered and the integration of sedentary groups and rural villages begins.

In this connection it should be mentioned that artifacts of great antiquity have been found in Mexico, as for example those from Cañada Marfil, Guanajuato; Río Juchipila, Zacatecas; and Cerro de las Palmas, Tacubaya, D.F. (dating to the Archaeolithic period). There is much evidence to prove the existence of hunters of Pleistocene fauna, such as the finds at San Joaquín, Lower California; Puntita Blanca, Sonora; Rancho Weicker, Durango; Cerro del Tecolote, Jalisco; Santa Isabel Ixtapan and

Tepexpan, Mexico (all from the Lower Cenolithic). Materials left by groups of gatherers of Upper Cenolithic and Proto-neolithic times have been found in Cueva Espantosa, Coahuila; Laguna Chapala, Lower California; Coxcatlán, Puebla; Santa Marta, Chiapas; Chicoloapan, Mexico, and elsewhere.

A large panel painted by Iker Larrauri shows the fauna of the Pleistocene, among which we find the mastodon, woolly mammoth or elephant, long-horned bison, American horse, bear, sabre-toothed tiger, sloth, giant armadillo, vicuña, and others. In front of this and inside a large pit is to be seen the reconstruction of a mammoth found at Santa Isabel Ixtapan showing also the associated tools.

The hunting of mammoth at Tepexpan has been reconstructed in a diorama based on data obtained from archaeological digging, from which it is clear that hunters surrounded these animals on the marshy shores of lakes in the Valley of Mexico and then attacked with spears and sharp lances; the monsters were finished off with maces and the carcass was cut up.

In this hall is also exhibited the fossil bone carving of Tequisquiac, a site in the north of the Valley of Mexico famous for the large quantity of fossil remains found there. This fragment of a vertebra, identified as that of an extinct type of camel, predecessor of the llama of South America, had been roughly *Ill. 7* carved to give it the appearance of the head of a coyote or some other canine. It is reckoned to be about 14,000 years old and is one of the earliest examples of American art.

The period of the nomadic hunters was followed by an era of food-gatherers who were established mainly in the north of the Republic, but penetrated as far south as Puebla, Oaxaca, and even Chiapas, as is evidenced by numerous finds in those areas. It was from these people that the Incipient Agriculturists developed, and after a long period of experimentation with certain plants which had previously been gathered they were able to lead a sedentary existence, with the result that the first villages were formed.

On display are stone querns and mullers for grinding seeds and wild fruits, scrapers, mortars and pestles; stone vessels, awls, tanged projectile points, nets, bags, etc. corresponding to the food-gathering stage. Some of the plants which were first gathered wild and later cultivated are also shown – among them corn, squash, chilli, *zapote*, avocado, amaranth, gourds, and cotton. These were already being used around 5000 B C.

Round about 2500 B C more advanced agriculture was introduced in Mexico as well as in many other parts of the American continent. This brought into existence villages, and led to the first steps being taken in pottery-making, in flaking and polishing stone implements, in weaving and basketry, as well as to the introduction of the cult of the dead. On these foundations the Preclassic cultures were built.

7 Fossil vertebra of a llama fashioned to resemble the head of a coyote. Bone. Tequisquiac, State of Mexico. Height: 13 cm. Lithic: 10,000 to 12,000 B C

The Preclassic Period in the Central Highlands

This hall was planned to show the development of the Preclassic or Formative cultures in the Central Highlands, a region comprising the Valley of Mexico and the States of Morelos, Mexico, Puebla, and Tlaxcala.

In general this horizon in Mesoamerica is characterized by a completely sedentary existence of agricultural groups, the introduction and development of pottery, the construction of dwellings, and a cult of the dead with advanced funerary practices. The cultural patterns in time led to more skilled craftsmen, the erection of the first temple bases, and the foundation of religion and a priestly caste. At the same time there began to take form a system of numbering, the calendar, hieroglyphic writing, and a technically advanced art, all of which later influenced other peoples.

Within the framework of this gradual evolution or cultural progress the Preclassic horizon has been divided into Lower, Middle, and Upper periods, to which can be added a transitional or Protoclassic period, with several features that would later distinguish the emerging civilizations of Mesoamerica.

The Lower Preclassic (1700–1300 BC) is characterized by the predominance of small rural communities comprising a limited number of huts built of perishable materials, and by the existence of two distinct types of pottery, consisting of vessels having round and flat bottoms, respectively. The former are associated with the Central Highlands, the latter with the Gulf Coast. At this stage the groups were distributed over an area extending from the Valley of Mexico and bordering states as far as the Gulf Coast and Chiapas, inhabiting the sites of El Arbolillo, Zacatenco, Tlatilco, Ajalpan, Izúcar, La Venta, San Lorenzo, El Trapiche, Chiapa de Corzo, and others.

In the Middle Preclassic period (1300–800 BC) agricultural communities move in the direction of a more densely populated type of village or town – made up of huts built over platforms of earth covered with stone, and tamped earth or slab floors – and develop local variations in both traditions of pottery. On the Gulf Coast, however, Olmec culture was by now integrated and had acquired considerable strength, with widespread influence, particularly over groups in the Central Highlands. During this period Copilco, Gualupita, Chalcatzingo, Viejón, Pánuco, Mazatán, Uaxactún, Kaminaljuyú, El Opeño, and other sites appear in addition to those previously mentioned.

The Upper Preclassic (800–200 BC) marked the apogee of the village groups, when small unplanned ceremonial centres make their first appearance, characterized by temple bases some of which contain tombs. The priesthood and a formalized religion also took shape, there were marked advances in scientific knowledge, principally of an astronomical and mathematical character, and in technology. Settlements now multiplied rapidly, among them Cuicuilco, Ticomán, Tlapacoya, Tres Zapotes, Remojadas, Monte Albán, Izapa, Tikal, Edzná, and Dzibilchaltún, to mention but a few.

Finally, in the Protoclassic period (200 BC–AD 200) a number of features which will later distinguish the Maya, Zapotec, Central Veracruz, and perhaps Huastec and Teotihuacán civilizations, can already be recognized. Among these are a precise technique of working stone, the erection of stelae and altars associated with them; the calendar and a system of numbering using dots and bars; the god of rain with recognizable attributes; fresco-type painting on vessels and tombs; tetrapod vessels with mammiform legs; labial and basal mouldings on pottery.

The first case exhibits pottery and figurines from the Lower Preclassic in the Valley of Mexico, with pieces from El Arbolillo, Tlatilco, and Zacatenco. Among the former are large jars for storing water and seeds, composite-silhouette bowls with incised decoration, jars with flaring sides, plates and other simple forms, with round bottoms; mostly monochrome, they are painted black, white, dark brown, chestnut-brown, and reddish brown. The figurines – all representing women – were made with an *appliqué* technique; these constitute Tradition C of the Central Highlands.

Ill. 8

The continuity of pottery during the Middle Preclassic period is shown next, using vessels with a polished surface of red, or white on red, as examples. At the same time emphasis is placed on the introduction of the Olmec pottery tradition from the Gulf Coast, characterized by vases, plates, gourd-shaped bowls and bottles; the latter have flat bottoms, adorned with feline or geometric motifs, and use decorative techniques of finger-nail marking, rocker stamping, textile impressions, excising, etc.

Ill. 12

The pottery of the Olmecs – in polished black, grey, white, black with white spots, or white with black spots, and even with negative decoration – gradually becomes mixed with the local ceramic styles, whereby the pottery of some sites in the Valley of Mexico, principally Tlatilco and Tlapacoya, becomes enriched. At this stage phytomorphic and zoomorphic bottles, dishes with spouts, stirrup-spout vessels, anthropomorphic receptacles, and other forms appear; among the colours and techniques used are red on white, red on brown, orange and yellowish lacquer, white with negative painting, and painting on dry stucco.

Ill. 13

With the arrival of the Olmecs a new type of figurine is also introduced into Central Mexico, characterized by a trapezoidal and enlarged mouth – resembling that of a child or a jaguar – and facial features formed by incising and punctuation. Other types continue to develop in the Highlands and become inter-mixed, resulting in many new types of figurines in the Middle Preclassic. These give us some indication of what the people of those times were like, how they dressed and adorned themselves, and of their daily life. One show-case contains a variety of figurines: men and women who are tall and short, thin or fat, some with special attributes such as cranial deformation, dental

Ill. 9

Ills. 10,   mutilation, a shaven head, tattooing, body and facial painting.
14, 4   The use of loin-cloths, short skirts, sandals, hats, turbans, ear-
plugs, necklaces, pyrite mirrors, and many other items of
clothing and adornment, is also evidenced by the pottery.

The visitor is next introduced to the economic aspects of these
groups, whose basic sustenance came from the agricultural
production of maize, squash, beans, and chilli, supplemented by
hunting, fishing, and gathering. In support of this are exhibited
cf. Ill. 57   vessels from the Middle Preclassic, representing squashes,
Ill. 13   rabbits, ducks, frogs, turtles, birds, and other animals.

Thanks to their technology these groups succeeded in
adapting themselves perfectly to their environment. By way of
illustration there are examples of their artifacts, such as stone
mortars and *metates* for pounding seeds and grinding maize;
projectile points for hunting; bone awls and needles for making
clothing; stone axes for clearing forests and working wood, as
well as scrapers and polishers.

In the section relating to religion we see that the groups in
the Valley of Mexico practised a fertility cult, related to natural
phenomena and fecundity, for which female figurines were
Ill. 15   modelled in clay with a view to propitiating gods who controlled the harvests. When Central Mexico came under Olmec
influence a jaguar deity related to the rain was adopted there,
soon becoming fused with an aquatic serpent to result in a sort
of celestial dragon that was later to evolve into the god of
water.

In their magico-religious capacity the wizards or magicians
took part in agricultural festivities wearing masks that depicted
Ill. 11   animals or human beings. Dancers of both sexes, acrobats,
hunchbacks, and ball-players attended these festivals and con-
Ill. 16   tributed to the entertainment; so did musicians with drums,
rattles, whistles, and so forth, and some of these instruments of
their trade are on view.

Finally, in this same section of the Middle Preclassic there are
choice pieces of pottery and figurines to illustrate the art of the
period. A burial at Tlatilco with its offerings serves to demon-

strate the cult of the dead. In this connection it is pertinent to note the custom of wrapping the deceased in mats or blankets and placing them, in either an extended or a flexed position, inside pits dug in the ground; the bodies were sprinkled with red paint or cinnabar and accompanied with offerings of food and personal objects for use in the hereafter.

The section devoted to the Upper Preclassic begins by showing the progress which had by then been made in technology, enabling platforms and temple bases to be built. On display are planes for levelling floors and walls, plumbs, hammers, chisels for cutting stone, and stone polishers; all of which points to the existence of stonecutters, masons, and others dedicated to the emergent architecture.

Pottery of the period reveals a predominance of polychrome and negative decoration, fresco-style painting, ornamental *Ill. 18* supports, painting outlined by incising, and ring bases. The pottery of Chupícuaro, Guanajuato is outstanding and influenced the ware of other groups, enriching their forms and decoration.

Among the exhibits are vessels in red on brown, white on red, black and red on cream, polished red, white and red on brown, polychrome pieces with the addition of negative decoration, and other variants. Figurines of the period are displayed together with traditional ones from Western Mexico.

With the appearance of small ceremonial centres and temple bases the worship of certain deities begins and a priestly caste emerges; illustrating these religious beliefs are representations of Huehueteotl – god of fire – conceived as an old hunchback who carries a brazier on his back, and antecedents of Tlaloc – *Ill. 17* god of rain – whose effigy is modelled on the neck of some bottles.

Illustrated on a panel is the evolution of architecture during the Upper Preclassic period, beginning with the simple platforms and huts of the Cerro del Tepalcate, followed by the superposing of platforms – as in the first stepped bases of Cuicuilco – built on a circular plan, first in clay and later of

37

stone, and developing later into the pyramidal base of Tlapacoya, which was to serve as an inspiration to the builders of the Pyramids of the Sun and of the Moon at Teotihuacán.

Inside the temple base at Tlapacoya three stone tombs with roofs of basalt slabs were found in which persons of importance had been buried, accompanied by hundreds of vessels, figurines, pieces of basketwork, and ornaments. The vessels, whose diverse shapes and decoration testify to the originality of the potters of this site, are given special prominence.

Ceramics from other Upper Preclassic and Protoclassic sites found in Zacatenco, Ticoman, Cuanalan, and Teotihuacán are to be seen in the last show-case. In general the forms are simple: red tripod bowls, plates, effigy vessels, and cylindrical vases, with negative or punctate decoration. Various types of figurines from sites all over Mesoamerica enable the visitor to distinguish different regions and Preclassic cultures. The over-all achievements of these cultures, which were ultimately to lead to the civilization of Teotihuacán, are also outlined here.

Outside the hall, in the adjoining garden, is set up a scale model of the small circular structure at Cuicuilco, which was built by superposing great basalt slabs, forming a sort of cupola or vaulted enclosure. There can be no doubt that the structure, which has an entrance passage and whose inner walls are painted with spiral or serpentine designs in red, was used for religious ceremonies.

8 Woman with
child in her arms.
Clay. Tlapacoya,
State of Mexico.
Height: 17 cm.
Lower Preclassic

10 (*right*) Hollow head with features of child, shaven and showing mutilated teeth. Clay. Tlatilco, State of Mexico. Height: 16 cm. Middle Preclassic. Olmec influence

11 (*right, below*) Contortionist or acrobat. Clay. Tlatilco, State of Mexico. Height: 22 cm. Middle Preclassic. Olmec influence

9 Priest wearing tiger skin. Clay. Atlihuayán, Morelos. Height: 21 cm. Middle Preclassic. Olmec influence

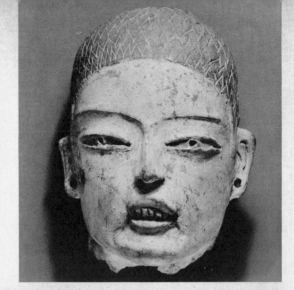

12 *(left)* Vase decorated with jaguar faces. Clay. Tlapacoya, State of Mexico. Height: 12 cm. Middle Preclassic. Olmec influence

13 *(left)* Vase in form of fish. Clay. Tlatilco, State of Mexico. Height: 13 cm. Middle Preclassic. Olmec influence

14 Hollow figure with shaven head and perhaps tattooed. Clay. Tlatilco, State of Mexico. Height: 31 cm. Middle Preclassic

15 Figurines of women with two faces and two heads respectively on a single body. Clay. Tlatilco, State of Mexico. Height: 6 and 11 cm. Middle Preclassic

16 *(right, above)* Figurines representing a magician or wizard, a musician with drum, and dancers. Clay. Tlatilco, State of Mexico. Height: 12, 8, 10 and 10 cm. Middle Preclassic

17 *(right)* The old god or god of fire (Huehueteotl) with brazier on his back. Clay. Cuicuilco, D.F. Height: 13 cm. Upper Preclassic

18 Vessels decorated with fresco painting. Clay. Tlapacoya, State of Mexico. Height: 22 and 14 cm. Upper Preclassic

Teotihuacan

In the midst of night
Before the break of light and day,
The gods assembled,
Holding council
Yonder in Teotihuacán.

Codex Matritensis

The cultural history of Teotihuacán dates back to the Upper Preclassic period, that is, 500 BC or earlier. At that time there were scattered villages in the Valley of Mexico whose populations practised agriculture, made pottery, and built crude temple bases.

At some stage between 200 BC and AD 150, these people began to concentrate upon a certain spot in the centre of the Valley. They built the Pyramids of the Sun and Moon, following the general lines of Preclassic architecture but on a monumental scale, giving them a stucco veneer and orienting them by the cardinal points.

With the passage of time, Teotihuacán developed a number of distinctive attributes that set it apart from other contemporary cultures. The characteristic *talud* and *tablero* (slope-and-panel) construction began to be used in architecture. The Temple of Quetzalcoatl (the plumed serpent), whose façade is formed of a stone mosaic and polychrome stucco was erected, and buildings such as the so-called *Subterráneos* and Temple of Agriculture, in which the first realistic mural paintings appear.

The new priestly caste governed society and promoted learning; it actively supported the crafts and encouraged worship of the gods, in particular Tlaloc and Chalchiutlicue who are related to water, and Huehueteotl, god of fire. At the same time monumental sculpture and pottery take shape, and trade

47

relations extend as far as Oaxaca and the Gulf Coast. These developments, occurring between AD 150 and 350, mark the beginning of urbanism, as exemplified by the growth of this important city of Teotihuacán.

The years between AD 350 and 650 see the floruit of Teotihuacán. The ceremonial centre is laid out with a north-south axis – represented by the Avenue of the Dead – and along its sides are aligned pyramidal temple bases and palaces for families of high rank. Great plazas such as that of the Moon and the Ciudadela (Fortress) are built for religious festivals. Residential zones and others for artisans are established, while near the periphery of the great city the huts occupied by the common people multiply.

Mural painting exalts the religious concepts of the Teotihuacanos, as the pantheon of deities grows larger. A remarkable increase in scientific knowledge leads to the invention of the calendar, hieroglyphic writing, and a system of numbering, while advances are made in astronomy and herbal medicine. All this is accompanied by an upsurge in commerce, with the result that Teotihuacán becomes the dominant cultural site in the Central Highlands, exerting considerable influence over neighbouring peoples.

Then around AD 650 Teotihuacán culture begins to decline. No more buildings of consequence are erected, the arts and crafts after a period of stagnation grow decadent, the priestly caste is no longer able to control the economy. It is at this stage that bands of more primitive people coming from the north, begin to invade the Valley of Mexico, and Teotihuacán falls an easy prey.

In the years that follow, these new arrivals burn and destroy much of the ceremonial centre, pilfer tombs and loot offerings, tear down buildings and ravage the city in other ways. But they also mingle with the survivors of the former population, occupying dwellings and adapting buildings to their needs. Though they have brought with them their own religion, these newcomers assimilate some of the local culture. This acculturation transforms them into 'artists and scholars'; in a word, they become 'Toltecs', and a new phase in the cultural growth of prehispanic Mexico is initiated.

A model of the Valley, taking in the ceremonial centre, puts the visitor in the picture and explains the ecological condition of the site.

He then passes on to a set of show-cases containing Teotihuacán pottery, which has been the means of establishing chronological periods corresponding to the various stages of its culture. First come examples of Teotihuacán I-A or Late Tzacualli, characterized by vessels shaped like flower vases, dishes with button supports, vases with images of Tlaloc, and other variants, all in brown with stick-polishing.

The Teotihuacán II or Miccaotli phase is represented by *Ills. 19, 21* jars, bowls, and cups with button supports; a number of amphorae with handles; and tripod vases and dish lids, in black or blackish brown, The next, transitional, phase produces pottery in red or light brown, red on yellow, and black, in the shape of bowls with solid conical supports and vases with flaring sides, often decorated by incising after the vessel was fired.

The most prominent forms of the ensuing Teotihuacán II-A or Early Tlamimilolpan phase include *candeleros* (candleholders), miniature vessels, goblets with spouts, shoe-shaped vessels, and vases with supports, embellished in various ways. This is followed by the Teotihuacán II-A-II or Late Tlamimilolpan phase, during which Thin Orange pottery attains a high degree of excellence and fresco painting is first introduced, as well as *champlevé* decoration principally on tripod vases with lids.

This leads on to pottery of the Teotihuacán III or Early Xolalpan phase; the Teotihuacán III-A or Late Xolalpan *Ills. 20, 22* period; the Teotihuacán IV-Metepec phase, taking in the *Ills. 23, 24* Coyotlatelco period, during which the site was abandoned. This entire classification lasts from 200 BC to AD 800, during which time Teotihuacán culture flourishes and declines.

Another section of the hall is devoted to the crafts and technology of the Teotihuacán people, as exemplified by archaeological objects recovered from the site. For the construction of their buildings, the stone was first hewn from the rock with wooden wedges and hammers, then cut and dressed with chisels and polishers. The masons also employed stone plumbs, polishers or planes for floors and walls, cords, rollers, and earthen ramps. The structures were generally covered with a finishing layer of lime plaster or stucco, to which paint and stone mosaics were also applied.

The Teotihuacanos were in the habit of adorning temples and the apartments of priests and nobles with frescoes, usually on religious themes. This was done by preparing the walls with a layer of stucco or lime plaster, and while it was still damp applying the colours diluted with water (fresco); sometimes the pigments were mixed with a resin or agglutinate, and used dry (tempera). Paint was also applied directly to stone, pottery, and figurines. The pigments were ground in mortars and mixed on palettes to obtain various tones, and then applied with fine and broad brushes. The basic colours, obtained from minerals, included red, blue, yellow, and black.

The lapidaries' tools were chisels made of serpentine, hammers, stone anvils, drills, borers, and polishers; they used abrasives such as sand and water to obtain highly polished surfaces on sculptures, masks, and the like.

From conch and other shells – acquired by trading from both the Gulf Coast of Mexico and the Pacific Coast – craftsmen fashioned beads for necklaces, pectorals, ear-plugs, and rings; large conch shells served as musical instruments. Bone and wood, though used less, were also worked with great skill.

Pottery was perhaps one of the most important crafts. They modelled vessels by hand or in moulds, the latter method enabling them to obtain series of objects for use in commercial exchange. In weaving they employed looms, spindles, and spindle whorls; by the use of needles, bodkins, and dyes, they produced various items of clothing out of cotton, maguey, and perhaps yucca. Out of the bark of the *amate* (a type of fig tree) they made paper.

In another part of the hall is to be seen a reproduction of the mural painting known as the 'Tlalocan' or 'Paradise of the god Tlaloc', a special heaven for warriors, ball-players, and persons who died by drowning or from dropsy. In it, the deceased appear as little 'portrait'-type figures, painted in pinks, blues, and yellows; they are shown swimming in the water of lagoons and rivers, chasing dragonflies and butterflies, singing and playing ball and other games. All are under the protection of Tlaloc, god of rain, who appears wearing rich apparel, a quetzal head-dress, and a mask over his face.

To be seen, too, is a replica of a corner of the Temple of Quetzalcoatl, in its original colours. The main features are serpents with precious plumes and snails and marine shells, alternating with huge masks of the rain god, all done in a polychrome stone mosaic. Near by are reproductions of mural paintings such as were found in buildings at Teotihuacán.

Among the outstanding pieces of sculpture exhibited is the stela from La Ventilla, made in four sections that can be taken apart. They are carved in low relief in the Central Veracruz style, the whole serving to mark off the field or court where the ball-game was played – in exactly the manner shown in one part of the 'Tlalocan'. This game was played with carved and painted wooden sticks, with which the player tried to propel the ball through the air from one end of the field to the other.

Another remarkable piece of sculpture is that of Chalchiut-licue, companion of Tlaloc and goddess of terrestrial waters. *Ill. 25* This was conceived as a block of stone, in keeping with the architectural style of Teotihuacán; it shows the goddess wearing a *huipil* (type of blouse) and decorated short skirt, a *quech-quemitl*, sandals, head-dress, ear-plugs, a necklace formed of three strands of beads, and bracelets.

Also on display are carvings of the god of fire, Huehueteotl, represented as an old man carrying a large brazier upon his *Ill. 27* head, and merlons with various decorative elements for the roofs of buildings. There is, too, a carving in the shape of a double human skull associated with the god of death, Mictlantecuhtli, the eyes and nose of which were originally inlaid with some precious material.

Large photo-murals and drawings of the ground-plans underline the architectural achievements of the Teotihuacanos, among them the Pyramid of the Sun and the Ciudadela. The Pyramid of the Sun was a temple base composed of sloping tiers with narrow treads, similar to Preclassic structures but on a monumental scale. It is 225 square metres at ground level and rises to a height of nearly 65 metres. Another frontage was added at a later date, using the typical Teotihuacán slope-and-panel technique.

The Ciudadela is a vast enclosure, 400 metres square, with small temple bases placed symmetrically upon the bordering platforms. Almost in the centre rises a large pyramidal base which was built against the Temple of Quetzalcoatl, practically covering it; before it stands an altar with four stairways. Both the enclosure, and the equally large Market, which faced the Ciudadela, were able to accommodate enormous crowds during religious festivals.

In its heyday Teotihuacán was divided into districts – some for artisans and some residential – each comprising a number of buildings with countless rooms and interior patios, but only a single entrance. That is, they were like apartment houses or blocks of rooms, containing streets and drainage systems.

The section of the hall devoted to minor sculpture attests the great technical skill of the stonecutters, who, equipped only with stone tools, were able to shape the serpentine, quartz, alabaster, jadeite, and other semi-precious materials into the desired form. On display are examples of their work such as *Ill. 28*   funerary masks, which perhaps were placed over the deceased's face; a human figurine with Olmec traits; a head with two circles, or *chalchihuites*, on the forehead; a small jaguar with *Ill. 26*   stylized features; a handsome vase with an effigy of Tlaloc, and much besides.

Finally, exhibited in a separate case, are choice examples of Teotihuacán pottery, outstanding among which are the Thin Orange ware, anthropomorphic vessels, dogs with legs extended, whistling jars in the shape of monkeys and other animals, jars and bowls sometimes decorated with fresco-type painting, vessels in the shape of a sandalled foot, cups and masks similar to those carved in stone.

Ills. 29, 31

Ill. 30

19 *(left)* Vessel in form of bird with adornments of marine conch and other shells. Clay. Height: 25 cm. Protoclassic. Teotihuacán II

20 *(left)* Vase with panel decorated in scrolls and interlacings. Clay. Height: 11 cm. Classic. Teotihuacán III

21 Brazier in form of temple with conical roof. Clay. Height: 30 cm. Protoclassic. Teotihuacán II

23 *(right)* Tripod vase with lid, decorated with shell disks. Clay. Height: 24 cm. Classic. Teotihuacán III

24 *(right, below)* Brazier with model of a temple and mask of a god in the interior. Clay. Height: 60 cm. Classic. Teotihuacán III–IV

22 Tripod with fresco decoration. Designs related to Tlaloc, god of rain. Clay. Height: 15 cm. Classic. Teotihuacán III

57

25 *(left)* Chalchiutlicue, or 'she of the jade skirt', goddess of water. Stone. Height: 3.20 m. Classic. Teotihuacán III

26 Vase with effigy of Tlaloc, god of rain. Stone. Height: 25 cm. Classic. Teotihuacán III

27 Huehueteotl, god of fire, with the face of an old man and brazier over his head. Stone. Height: 36 cm. Classic. Teotihuacán III

28 Funerary mask.
Stone. Height: 18 cm.
Classic. Teotihuacán III

29 *(right)* Human mask
with circular ear-plugs.
Clay. Height: 10 cm.
Classic. Teotihuacán III

30 *(below)* Thin
Orange jar of which
a seated human figure
forms a part.
Clay. Height: 21 cm.
Classic. Teotihuacán III

31 *(right, below)* Thin
Orange vessel of
which a reclining
human figure forms
a part. Clay.
Height: 12 cm.
Classic.
Teotihuacán III

The Toltecs

In truth the Toltecs were wise,
For they looked deeply into their own hearts.

By the time Teotihuacán had reached the height of its splendour and Monte Albán and El Tajín flourished in Oaxaca and Central Veracruz, the archaeological city of Xochicalco, Morelos, began its cultural development, which betrays influences from those more advanced groups and in which even elements of the Maya, the mathematical geniuses of Mesoamerica, are apparent.

Since the rise of Xochicalco, 'the house of flowers', was contemporary with the end of Teotihuacán and the beginning of the Toltecs in Tula, visitors to this hall are shown material from Xochicalco before they are introduced to the true Toltec culture.

Built on a large hill which was artificially reshaped by means of stepped terraces and retaining buttresses, the city of Xochicalco was provided with moats and various kinds of fortified structures. Within it are plazas surrounded by temple bases, altars, ball-courts, colonnades, caves adapted for astronomical observation, and other structures, many of them now in ruins.

Its principal temple base – known as Pyramid of the Plumed Serpent – reflects the architectural style of Teotihuacán, although here the panels have shrunk to cornices and the distance between them is greater. The decorative motifs – serpents adorned with plumes and sectioned snail shells – are, however, the same and the bas-reliefs in no way inferior to those at Teotihuacán. Within the curves of the serpent's body appear a series of seated, human figures, in the style of bas-reliefs on stelae and plaques of the Maya culture. Various hieroglyphs in Zapotec and Aztec styles also appear, one of which records the adjustment of the calendar needed at this site to make it accord with those of other groups.

Maya influence is evident in the ball-court, a structure in the form of a capital 'I' with stone rings embedded in the wall in a manner similar to that used at Uxmal and Chichen Itzá, Yucatán. From Xochicalco too comes a wonderful carving in the shape of a *guacamaya* in which the artist has succeeded in conveying the *Ill. 34* intrinsic nature of the bird and its solar symbolism by delineating a few essential features. Apropos the *guacamaya* (macaw), we should mention that in the ball-court in Copán, Honduras, these birds were also used as markers for the field.

Xochicalco is the source of other carvings; these include the so-called 'Palace Stone', bearing hieroglyphs and numerals which here again pertain to a calendar adjustment; the sculpture known as 'La Malinche' or 'The Indian Woman', portraying a goddess of vegetation; the image of a standing woman holding a disk or round vessel over her stomach; and three handsome stelae carved on all four sides with effigies of Tlaloc and of *Ill. 32* Quetzalcoatl, in a style combining Aztec, Zapotec, and Central Veracruz elements. Several of these pieces are on display.

Even the pottery from Xochicalco shows a connection with the Maya region, with Teotihuacán, and with the beginnings of Tula, as the orange, blackish, reddish, and other wares attest. Plain yokes, Mezcala-type figurines, shells from the Pacific, an alabaster vase with fresco decoration, and jadeite *Ill. 33* pectorals or plaques are among the many objects with affinities with the other groups that point to extensive trading having been carried on in those days.

The chronicler Fray Bernardino de Sahagún refers to people who settled in Tamoanchán, 'the place of the bird-serpent', where they composed the count of the days, of the nights, and of the years, which continued in use until the times of the Aztecs or Mexicas. Sahagún also relates how from Tamoanchán some groups went to Xomiltepec and then to the city of Teotihuacán, where they elected their respective rulers.

'And once the election of the lords had been held they all left, each lord being accompanied by the people who spoke his language, and each group was guided by its god. The Toltecs went always in front, followed by the Otomis who on arriving at Coatepec went no further . . . and the other peoples, such as the Toltecs and Aztecs and Nahuas . . . continued on their way through level country or high barren plains to discover lands. . . .'

These historic references seem to indicate that Tomoanchán could have been Xochicalco, since its principal temple base is decorated with plumed serpents, and the site called Xomiltepec or Jumiltepec is between that great centre and Teotihuacán. In Xochicalco too are found hieroglyphs referring to an adjustment of the Aztec, Maya, Zapotec, and perhaps Central Veracruz calendars; its sculptures, stelae, and certain other features also have affinities with these peoples.

From archaeological evidence and historic sources we know too that Teotihuacán was occupied by peoples of a lower cultural level around AD 650 or 700. The celebration of the Fifth Sun was held there, implying a change in religion, and the Annals of Cuauhtitlán in speaking of this event say that '. . . the name of this sun is Nahui Ollin (4 Movement); it is the one in which we live today . . . because the sun fell into the fires, in the divine oven of Teotihuacán . . . [and] it was the same sun of Topiltzin of Tollan [Tula], of Quetzalcoatl. Before this sun, his name was Nanahuatl, and he came from Tamoanchán.' That is to say, with this event the Toltec era began.

It would seem then that, as was the case at the fall of Teotihuacán, people arrived there who mingled with the existing population, imposed a new religion, adopted part of the culture of this great centre, and qualified as craftsmen, artists, and scholars. After some time they went to Tulancingo and later to Tula, Hidalgo, where they founded another city of 'Tollan', to which historic sources refer.

Pottery found at Tula begins with the Coyotlatelco type – from the end of Teotihuacán – which is characterized by simple bowls, cups, and tripod dishes painted in red on yellowish brown. From this derives the Mazapán pottery, distinguished by its dishes and bowls in a cream colour and with series of parallel wavy lines in red, made by using several brushes at the same time. Vessels in an orange colour were also produced and painted with broad brush-strokes in black on orange and brushed white. In addition, pottery was imported from other sites, including 'plumbate' ware with a hard metallic lustre, and cloisonné and polychrome ware of the Huasteca. *Ill. 36*

Figurines were made in moulds and are very flat, often painted in blue, red, yellow, white, and black, with the colour applied directly to the clay. Women, deities, and high-ranking individuals are represented, as well as warriors. *Ill. 35*

The Toltecs followed the urban model of the great city centres of the Classic, as well as sculptural styles of that time. However, they gradually developed features of their own which in turn influenced other groups.

Toltec buildings use the slope-and-panel system but the proportions are in inverse ratio to those of Teotihuacán. There is a ball-court similar to that of Xochicalco. The Toltecs decorated their temple bases and pillars with bas-reliefs. They further developed the concept of serpent columns which originated at Teotihuacán. They also adopted the decoration in the form of little drums or columns of the Maya Puuc period, as can be seen in the Palacio Quemado (Burned Palace) which is illustrated in a painted panel prominently displayed in the hall; there are in addition archaeological specimens by way of example.

Among the buildings in the centre of Tula are: the Temple of the Sun and the Temple of Tlahuizcalpantecuhtli which flank two sides of a large ceremonial plaza; a colonnade that communicates with the Palacio Quemado; a wall with serpents and sectioned snail shells; another plaza containing a ball-court, and remains of rooms and altars. In an adjoining zone there is a circular temple base dedicated to the god of wind, and a *tzompantli* or altar decorated with skulls.

The Temple of Tlahuizcalpantecuhtli, or god of the dawn, is the most important at Tula. It is composed of various super-posed tiers on the slope-and-panel principle, decorated with friezes in low relief showing coyotes, royal vultures, and eagles and tigers wearing necklaces, perhaps symbolizing the warrior or military orders. Upon a pyramidal base stood the temple itself, with two serpent columns forming the entrance and supporting the lintels, as well as four atlantean columns of stone and various square pillars decorated with warriors, which carried the roof.

The atlantean columns of Tula, one of which is on display in the hall, are 4·60 metres high and are formed of four sections joined together by a mortise-and-tenon system. They represent warriors wearing feather head-dresses, head-bands, ear-plugs, butterfly breastplates, short skirts held up by a belt which has a large disk at the back associated with the sun, and sandals with ankle-strap; in one hand they carry an *atlatl,* or spear-thrower, and in the other a sheaf of darts.

The Toltecs were in fact competent sculptors, both in low relief and in the round, as is evidenced by the so-called Chac-
Ill. 37   Mools – statues of reclining figures with raised head who bear a receptacle upon the stomach in which the sacrificial offering was placed. They symbolize the 'divine messenger' who carried the offering to the sun god. These figures were usually placed in front of altars.

Ills. 38,   To be seen also are: several characteristic examples of
39, 41   atlantean figures, carved in basalt and used to support stone tables or altars; tablets from the Coatepantli carved in low relief and depicting serpents devouring skeletal human beings, perhaps alluding to the disappearance of Venus as morning star and her transformation into the evening star; and the repro-duction of a bench decorated with a procession of richly attired warriors and priests. This latter was originally stuccoed and painted in various colours.

At Tula the Toltecs worshipped Quetzalcoatl, god of the planet Venus in both its morning and evening aspects, and the priests were named after this deity and wore his attributes. For this reason one of the important rulers of Tula was called Ce Acatl Topiltzin Quetzalcoatl; though he became a civilizing god-hero, he must not be confused with the god after whom he was named. The city had other rulers, including Huemac, under whom the floruit of the ceremonial centre came to an end. As such, the Toltec period had lasted from AD 900 to 1200.

In Tula's final stage, according to historic sources, some of its people scattered through Puebla and Tlaxcala, occupied Cholula, and conquered the Olmec-Xicalancas, who emigrated towards the Gulf Coast. The surviving population of Tula saw new groups of Chichimecs arrive, among them the hordes of Xolotl and later the Aztecs, who were the last to inherit a measure of their cultural knowledge and who gave them the name of 'Toltecs', meaning craftsmen and scholars.

Towards the far end of the hall are exhibited materials from Cholula, Puebla, whose history begins with the settlement there in the Preclassic of peoples who erected platforms, basic-ally of mud and stone; it then came under the influence of, or was colonized by, a Teotihuacán group, who left temple bases of the slope-and-panel type, one of them painted with frescoes showing grasshoppers.

All these structures were used as fill for subsequent building done by other groups; that is to say, they were covered over to erect the great pyramid of Cholula, a model of which is on exhibit. This imposing edifice was more than 400 metres square at the base and had at least three tiers whose total height was more than 60 metres. The church of Los Remedios was built over the pyramid in the early days after the Spanish Conquest.

In Cholula a beautiful polychrome ware was produced known as Cholultec or Mixtec-Puebla on account of its strong resemblance to the Mixtec pottery. Its forms include dishes, goblets with ring base, jars and bowls embellished with floral motifs, frets, skulls, human shin-bones, hieroglyphs, and geo-metric designs. Black, wine-red, grey, orange, and white were the favoured colours, which were used in various combinations.

32 Stela with face of Tlaloc, god of rain. Stone. Xochicalco, Morelos. Height: 1.49 m. Late Classic.

33 (right) Alabaster vase with fresco decoration forming a panel. Stone. Xochicalco, Morelos. Height: 1.49 m. Late Classic

34 (right) Head of guacamaya (macaw). Stone. Xochicalco, Morelos. Height: 55 cm. Late Classic

35 Figurines with paint applied directly to clay. Tlaloc priest, with a woman on either side. Clay. Height: 18, 20 and 15 cm. Early Postclassic

36 (left, below) Zoomorphic vessel of 'Tohil plumbate' type. Clay. Height: 16 cm. Early Postclassic

37 Chac-Mool. It represents the 'divine messenger' who received and carried to the Sun the offering of human sacrifice. Stone. Height: 66 cm. Early Postclassic

38, 39 Atlantean figure in the form of a warrior. Stone. Height: 1.15 m.
Early Postclassic

40 *(right)* Figure holding a banner. Stone. Height: 1.10 m. Early Postclassic

42 Human face with coyote head-dress. Clay and shell mosaic.
Height: 14 cm. Early Postclassic

41 *(left)* Atlantean figure, 'Colossus of Tula', in the form of a
warrior. Stone. Height: 4.60 m. Early Postclassic

44 Tablet with effigy of the god
Quetzalcoatl (the plumed serpent) or the
planet Venus. Stone. Height: 61 cm.
Early Postclassic

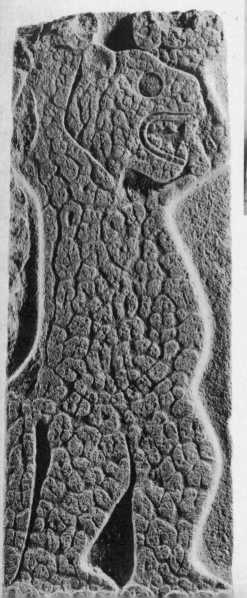

43 Tablet with relief of dancing jaguar.
Stone. Height: 1.26 m. Early Postclassic

The Mexica

As long as the world exists
The fame and glory of Mexico-Tenochtitlán
Will have no end.
　　　　　Memorials of Culhuacán

This hall, on the far side of the Museum's big patio, was conceived on a large scale so as to provide a proper background for the culture of the Mexica, or Aztecs, who founded Tenochtitlán, today Mexico City.

The Mexica were originally known as 'Chichimecs', on account of their nomadic habits; they emigrated from a legendary place called Aztlán or 'Place of Herons' – perhaps in the Bajío of Guanajuato – finally reaching the Valley of Mexico. During their wanderings they passed through Tula, at a time when the Toltec culture had come to an end, and later entered and settled other sites of the Valley of Mexico before reaching the environs of Chapultepec, today a wooded park within Mexico City.

At the outset the Mexica were subjugated by the Lords of Culhuacán – a neighbouring kingdom of Toltecs; after regaining their freedom, they wandered from place to place until they found refuge on a small barren island surrounded by water and reeds or cat's-tails. Here the prophecy of their god Huitzilopochtli was fulfilled, for on this island they saw an eagle devouring a serpent just as the deity had foretold. Accordingly, in 1325 they founded on this spot a modest town, destined to become the great Tenochtitlán.

At this time the Aztecs were under the rulership of Azcapotzalco, but their leaders Acamapichtli, Huitzilihuitl, and Chimalpopoca (1376–1427) began to develop the city, dividing it into districts or *calpullis* and organizing its society. Sometime later Itzcoatl, a great ruler and conqueror (1427–40) freed them from the yoke of Azcapotzalco, in which struggle he was aided by Netzahualcoyotl, Lord of Texcoco.

A period of maximum expansion and prosperity, particularly under the leadership of Moctezuma Ilhuicamina, Axayacatl, Tizoc, and Ahuizotl, ensued; Moctezuma Xocoyotzin was the ruler of this empire when the Spaniards arrived in 1519. After months of tenacious resistance against their assault, Tenochtitlán at last succumbed; in this, both the superiority of European arms and the help given to the Spaniards by certain indigenous groups – in their desire to throw off the Aztec yoke – played their part. Cuauhtemoc was the last Aztec ruler.

Ill. 46
Ill. 60
Ill. 47

The first exhibits in this hall are three choice and representative pieces of the Mexica culture: the great Ocelocuauhxicalli, a sculptured jaguar with a hollow place for depositing the hearts of sacrificial victims; the head of an Eagle Knight, symbolizing the military orders; and the Teocalli de la Guerra Sagrada (the Sacred War was an institution by which victims were obtained for sacrifice in the temples). These carvings symbolize the character of Aztec society, which was profoundly religious as well as militaristic.

Next, antecedents of this group are shown, in particular the settlement of the Xolotl Chichimecs in Tenayuca, where the architectural feature of twin temples – later adopted by the Aztecs – had its origin. The 'Tira de la Peregrinación' indicates the places where the Aztecs stayed on their travels from the time they left Aztlán until their arrival at Chapultepec.

There are panels showing how the Mexica culture spread, and giving information concerning the language they spoke, its relation to other languages, its geographic distribution, and so forth. Various realistic sculptures, both male and female, give a good idea of what these people looked like and the clothing they wore.

Ill. 48
The so-called 'Stone of Tizoc', a circular monolith 2·65 metres in diameter, commemorates the conquests of this ruler.

On it are carved fifteen scenes, each portraying two figures:
the conqueror Tizoc and the leader of the vanquished people,
who is held by the hair as a symbol of subjugation. A replica of
the Head-dress of Moctezuma, made of precious quetzal
feathers and embellished with gold, is also exhibited.

At the height of the Mexicas' prosperity the city of Tenochtitlán made great progress in urbanization. The island was
connected with the lake shores by wide avenues: that of
Ixtapalapa on the south, Tepeyac on the north, and Tacuba on
the west side. A network of canals allowed the passage of canoes,
and there were boulevards for pedestrians; sidewalks or dikes
adjoined the buildings. An earthen wall or dam kept the saline
water of Texcoco from mixing with the potable water of
Xochimilco and Chalco; at the same time an aqueduct coming
from Chapultepec supplied drinking water to the city, which
also had public fountains, a drainage system, and other important
urban works.

In the centre of the city was the ceremonial precinct, guarded
by a wall or *coatepantli* ornamented with large serpents; access
to it was limited to three avenues. Within this area rose the
Great Temple with its twin shrines dedicated to Tlaloc and
Huitzilopochtli; the Temple of Quetzalcoatl, with its circular
plan; the *tlachtli* or ball-court; the *tzompantli*; the *temalacatl*,
an altar where gladiatorial combats were held, and other
temples and civil and religious structures.

Around the ceremonial precinct were located the palaces or
dwellings of nobles and functionaries, mostly of masonry and
surrounded by orchards and gardens. In this area there were also
other buildings such as the Tlacochcalli or arsenal, the Cuicacalli
or house of song, the Calmecac or school for sons of noblemen,
and the Telpochcalli or school for sons of plebeians. This
imposing urban complex was greatly admired by the Spaniards.
A large model and a mural in colour vividly convey what the
great city of Tenochtitlán looked like in its heyday.

Another section of the hall illustrates the economy of the
Mexica, which was based on agriculture, hunting, fishing, and

gathering, although it was war, the exaction of tributes, and trade, that made it possible to maintain the evergrowing population. Owing to the shallowness of the lake, the Mexica were forced to create *chinampas* – often called 'floating gardens' – platforms supported by piles and covered with mud from the lake bottom. These eventually took root, thus adding more territory where the Mexica could live and plant crops which, thanks to the fertility of the mud and constant irrigation from the lake waters, produced more than one crop a year.

Tributes from subject peoples in countless territories furnished Tenochtitlán with food and manufactured articles, including highly prized feathers, gold, turquoise, skins, copal, tobacco, honey, jade, salt, banners, arrows, and cacao. Through trade they also acquired both raw materials and luxury items of an exotic character, greatly esteemed by ruler and nobles. Thus from tropical regions Tenochtitlán imported fruits and animals, jaguar and deer skins, quetzal feathers from the Highlands of Guatemala and Chiapas; cacao from Soconusco; gold and silver from Central America, jade from Guerrero and the Usumacinta region; woven cloth from the Huasteca, and liquidambar. The greater part was brought by *pochtecas* or merchants, and sold or exchanged in the city's markets.

A diorama shows the market of Tlatelolco; this was one of the most important of its time, although examples were to be found also in Azcapotzalco, Tacuba, and Tenochtitlán. In these markets, or *tianguis*, judges or officials were charged with maintaining order, setting prices, attending to complaints, and preventing robberies. Vendors occupied permanent pitches, exhibiting their wares in rows of stalls arranged like streets. As currency they used gold-dust, cacao beans, copper axes, shells, precious feathers, and other items. Another part of the hall contains reproductions of drawings from the Florentine and Mendocine Codices, illustrating Mexica customs, such as those surrounding birth, family education, marriage, and death.

In the social and political organization of the Aztecs a State Council was made up of nobles and members of the ruling family; next came the Tlacatecuhtli or Tlatoani, who was the principal lord and military and political chief of the Empire. Below him was the Cihuacoatl, or general of the military forces, who at times also held the position of High Priest. Next in line came the *pillis* or nobles, who had administrative duties and served as judges, magistrates, priests, merchants, mayors, etc. The lowest social strata comprised the *macehualli, mayeques, tamemes,* and others. The *macehualli* or commoners devoted themselves to the crafts; *mayeques* were from conquered groups and held a position similar to that of serfs in feudal Europe, and the *tamemes* or carriers were slaves.

From here the visitor passes on to the section devoted to religion; this was polytheistic and recognized both local gods and deities adopted from conquered peoples. Prominent in the Aztec pantheon were the gods Huitzilopochtli, 'Lord of the Universe'; Tezcatlipoca, god of night; Huehueteotl, god of fire; Tlazolteotl, goddess of fertility; Macuilxóchitl, god of games; Coatlicue, mother of the gods and earth goddess; and Mictlantecuhtli, god of death.

These deities had well-defined attributes and governed or presided over special regions of the universe; they were associated with certain colours and symbolic numbers, cardinal points, and various heavens. Great celebrations were held in their honour on dates established by the religious calendar, accompanied by sacrifices, music, dances, games, and other diversions.

A number of gods upon whom agriculture was dependent are portrayed: Tlaloc, god of rain, and Xilonen, goddess of corn; Ehecatl, god of wind, with his buccal mask in the shape of a duck's bill; Quetzalcoatl, associated with the planet Venus; and Tonatiuh, god of the sun. Also shown are replicas of sacrificial knives adorned with mosaics of shell and turquoise, the stone on which the victim was laid for sacrifice, and the *cuauhxicalli* or stone box in which the heart of the sacrificial victim was placed.

Occupying a privileged place near the centre of the hall is the statue of the goddess Coatlicue, of the serpent skirt, mother of *Ill. 54* gods and of man. She is portrayed as a beheaded woman from whose neck two large serpent-heads emerge. She wears a necklace made up of human hearts, two hands with palms turned outwards, and a skull containing lifelike eyes. Her petticoat or skirt is a mass of serpents whose bodies are interlaced like a rhomboidal keyboard. She wears a sash made of two serpents knotted in front; serpents that resemble enormous claws take the place of hands. Her feet are like eagle's talons with the nails grasping the earth.

This awesome statue represents an abstraction of the religious creed of the Mexica, since Coatlicue was the goddess of birth and death, she who gave and took away life, personifying the duality of the human being. Hence the two large serpent-heads that emerge from the neck, facing each other. Her necklace symbolizes life and death for the sacrificial victim, the giving and taking away of existence as an offering to the gods so as to conserve order in the universe. Her petticoat symbolizes the earth, and her talons or feet penetrate the world of the dead – represented below in the form of a relief of Tlaltecuhtli, the god associated with death, the earth, and water.

Ill. 45 There is too a statue of Coyolxauhqui, the moon goddess, who is beheaded by her brother the sun as he rises triumphant each morning. The goddess is represented with her hair covered in balls of down, and on her cheeks she wears golden bells from which her name in Nahuatl is derived; solar earplugs adorn her ears and a dangler is suspended from her nose. Her eyes are half open as in death.

Also exhibited are two monumental clay braziers from Tlatelolco, which were placed on top of the pyramidal bases and in front of the temples for burning copal; likewise two
cf. Ill. 40 flagpole-holders sculptured in stone in which banners or insignia were placed to indicate the month and announce festivities in honour of the presiding god.

Ill. 50 Upon a marble platform is the Sun Stone, commonly known as the 'Aztec Calendar'. This carving in the form of a disk is a votive monument to the sun, since the face of Tonatiuh appears in the centre, surrounded by the symbol for Nahui Ollin (4 Movement). Inside this are shown the four suns or cosmogonic worlds which had preceded Aztec times, namely Nahui Ehecatl (4 Wind), Nahui Ocelotl (4 Tiger), Nahui Atl (4 Water), and Nahui Quiahuitl (4 Rain of Fire). Encircling these is a band containing the hieroglyphs of the twenty days that comprised the indigenous month. Other bands show the solar rays, precious stones, symbols for blood, flowers, and elements related to the cult of the sun, as well as the two fire-serpents which indicate the cyclic and cosmic order.

The hall also contains the great statue of Xiuhcoatl, the star-crowned fire-serpent who led the sun in its path through the celestial vault. A statue of the Cihuateteos, who are patron goddesses of women who die in labour, and a *tzompantli* or altar adorned with skulls are among the monuments associated with the theme of death. *Ill. 49*

Religion and learning at this period were in the hands of the priestly caste, a hierarchy in which each individual had his specific function. Thus there were priests in charge of worship and ceremonies, festivals, sacrificial rites, marriages and baptisms; others to predict the future for new-born babies, to teach and promote learning, including mathematics, the calendar, astronomical observations, astrology, botany and herbal medicine, and the arts of hieroglyphic writing, literature and poetry, architecture, making of codices, and so forth.

In the field of the arts, the Mexica produced their own codices painted on leather or paper made of *maguey* and containing religious, calendrical, historic, geographic, and sometimes genealogical data; they developed feather-work; carved wood and hard materials such as obsidian, rock-crystal, and alabaster; modelled clay figurines and pottery vessels; and produced excellent sculpture, above all in the form of deities and animals. *Ill. 59* *Ill. 52* *Ill. 51*

One show-case contains pieces of minor sculpture including obsidian masks, stone boxes with fresco painting and figures of gods and animals; another shows ceramic ware produced by the Mexica potters, mainly in black on orange, black on *Ill. 57*

83

Ill. 53 wine-red, and polychrome using black, red, white, and yellow, together with Mixtec pottery – patronized by this group – with motifs similar to those of the codices.

Ill. 58 On display also are musical instruments, such as beautifully carved *teponaxtlis* (horizontal wooden drums with two tongues cut into the sounding-board); ocarinas; conch shells; flutes; and turtle-carapace drums. Jewellery, obsidian carvings, and feather-work make up other exhibits.

Ill. 55 Before leaving this hall the visitor will come to the statue of the god Xochipilli, god of flowers and song, of love and poetry, wearing a mask over his face and seated on a throne decorated with flowers and *chalchihuites* (jade disks); the god Macuilxóchitl or 5 Flower, god of games, represented as a man emerging from

Ill. 56 a turtle carapace; and the drum from Malinalco, made of wood and ornamented with carvings in low relief featuring an eagle and other decorative elements.

45 Coyolxauhqui, the moon goddess, beheaded by her brother the Sun.
Stone. Height: 72 cm. Late Postclassic

46 *(left, above)* Receptacle shaped like a jaguar (Ocelocuauhxicalli), in which hearts of sacrificial victims were placed. Stone. Height: 93 cm. Late Post-classic

47 *(centre, above)* Commemorative monument known as 'Teocalli de la Guerra Sagrada' (Temple of the Sacred War). Stone. Height: 1.23 m. Late Postclassic

48 *(right, above)* Detail of the 'Stone of Tizoc', which depicts that ruler's conquests. Stone. Height: 93 cm. Late Postclassic

49 *(left)* Xiuhcoatl, the fire-serpent, whose crest is adorned with stars. Stone. Height: 2.15 m. Late Post-classic

50 Sun Stone or 'Aztec Calendar', with hieroglyphs of days, months and suns or cosmogonic periods. Stone. Diameter 3.60 m. Late Postclassic

51 Sculpture in form of grasshopper. Stone. Length: 48 cm. Late Postclassic

52 Vase shaped in part like a monkey. Obsidian. Height: 14 cm. Late Postclassic

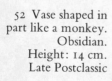

88

53 Pitcher decorated in green on dark brown. Clay. Height: 28 cm. Late
Postclassic

55 Xochipilli ('Prince of Flowers'), god of music, song and love, seated cross-legged on his throne. Stone. Height: 77 cm. Late Postclassic

56 *Huehuetl* (musical drum), decorated with carved eagles, Wood. Malinalco. State of Mexico. Height: 88 cm. Late Postclassic

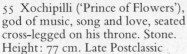

54 (*left*) Coatlicue, or 'she of the serpent skirt', goddess of the earth and creator of man, patron of life and death. Stone. Height: 2.57 m. Late Postclassic

57 Sculpture representing a squash. Stone. Length: 31 cm. Late Postclassic

58 *Teponaxtle*, or horizontal drum, decorated with human figure carved in relief. Wood. Height: 15 cm. Length: 60 cm Late Postclassic

59 Figure of a young woman. Wood. Height: 50 cm. Late Postclassic

60 Head of 'Eagle Knight'. Stone. Height: 31 cm. Late Postclassic

The Cultures of Oaxaca

Unlike the halls devoted to particular cultures of the Central Highlands, this one was planned to show the cultural development of a region, in this case Oaxaca. It is divided into two sections, one concerned with the Zapotecs the other with the Mixtecs – whose descendants still inhabit this area.

Zapotec culture reached its peak in the central valleys of the State of Oaxaca – in Etla, Tlacolula, and Zimatlán in particular – while that of the Mixtecs evolved in the high mountain ranges or 'cloud country', as their name in the Nahuatl or Aztec language implies.

The initial exhibit in this hall is a museographic display showing the most characteristic aspects of these two cultures: the Zapotecs' elaboration of clay urns with representation of gods. A beautiful urn showing the goddess 13 Serpent illustrates this. A fragment of frieze adorned with frets from Mitla, a Mixtec site, shows the stone mosaics which the Mixtecs used for decorating the façades of buildings.

A topographical map of the State of Oaxaca shows the regional features which influenced the evolution of these two cultures, and on it are marked many of their archaeological sites.

Effigies of the rain god as he was depicted in various periods give the visitor a good idea of the cultural evolution of the Zapotecs. In a similar way the pottery is set out in chronological order, based on archaeological typology.

It should be mentioned in this connection that the origin of of the Zapotecs is linked with the Olmec culture of the Gulf Coast as well as with groups in southern Chiapas – the proto-Maya. This is perhaps why historic sources tell us the Zapotecs were descended from lions and tigers, animals closely related to the jaguar, the favourite animal of the Olmecs which served both as a deity and a totem for these people.

From archaeological evidence we know that around 900 B C the Olmecs of the Gulf Coast began to spread through the region of the Tehuantepec Isthmus occupying such places as Juchitán and Zope Lagune; at the same time others moved gradually towards Puerto Angel, Huamelulpan, and Monte Albán. These first cultural manifestations therefore show a strong Olmec influence, to be seen in the building known as 'Los Danzantes' (The Dancers), in murals, hieroglyphs, ceramics, and other artistic works.

The pottery of the Monte Albán I period (900–300 B C), which occupies a large show-case, is characteristically mono-chrome, that is to say the vessels are basically in tones of black, white, and grey. To the fore are receptacles showing swimmers *Ill. 63* and human or animal representations with Olmec traits, often with a simple spout. Also displayed are shoe-shaped vessels, *Ill. 62* dishes, bottles, braziers with typically Olmec faces, and minia-ture vessels representing a variety of animals including fish, frogs and snails.

Next, the visitor is shown a reproduction of part of the wall from 'Los Danzantes' at Monte Albán, as well as original panels from this building, in which Olmec influence is marked; the beginnings of architecture in this ceremonial centre can here be studied. The two tiers of the structure were covered with a series of large panels arranged both vertically and horizontally, the former engraved with figures in dynamic postures – the so-called 'Danzantes' – and the latter showing swimmers.

Hieroglyphs and numerals appear on the majority of the panels and it is therefore assumed that a calendar had already been invented and that arithmetic was among their accom-plishments. From these same panels, too, can be deduced the customs of the group, such as shaving the head or leaving large locks of hair; wearing scanty or no clothing, but adorning themselves with ear-plugs and other ornaments; and indulging in tattooing or scarification.

Another show-case contains pottery from Monte Albán II (300–100 BC) in which certain influences from the South are apparent in the mammiform supports, labial and basal mouldings, fresco decoration, negative painting, spool pot-stands, and tetrapod vessels – all frequently found also at sites in the Maya region. Genuine urns are introduced and various new pottery shapes. Among the more arresting exhibits are boxes with lids and incised and painted decoration; a spool pot-stand in the form of a spinal column; and a model of a temple with columns and a *guacamaya* (macaw) in the centre, symbolizing the sun.

Ill. 65

During this period the structure known as Mound J at Monte Albán was built; used for astronomical observations, it was decorated with panels which recall those of the 'Danzantes' building. Funerary architecture too was developed; the dead, accompanied by offerings, were placed inside box tombs and tombs with antechambers and vaulted ceilings. Clay urns showing deities became common, and through these we know that Cocijo, god of rain, Huehueteotl, god of fire, a god wearing a bird mask over his face, and a bat god related to death were already being worshipped.

The bat god is exquisitely rendered on a jade mask composed of various pieces expertly joined together. Here great technical skill in the carving of this material has produced a work of art whose high quality adds to its religious significance. There are examples of clay sculpture including an enormous jaguar with fresco decoration and necklace, and an urn with a deity wearing a kind of helmet shaped like a broad-billed bird.

Ill. 61

Ill. 64

The ensuing period at Monte Albán really represents a transitional stage on the way to the Zapotec culture (100 BC– AD 200), and some influence from Teotihuacán is apparent in the pottery; it is characterized by flower vases and *candeleros* (candle-holders), stirrup-spouted jars, incense-burners, and urns of various types, some depicting Tlaloc.

Separate show-cases contain pottery from the floruit of the Zapotecs – Monte Albán periods IIIA and IIIB (AD 200–800).

Quite outstanding are vases in the shape of a tiger's or bat's claw, bowls and vases with panels of hieroglyphs, figures of *Ill. 69* women wearing *quechquemitls, enredos* (shawls which have been *Ill. 66* twisted to form a head-covering), lids for braziers and urns *Ill. 68* depicting gods. One of these shows Xipe Totec carrying a stick in one hand and a human head in the other.

It is through such urns that we have come to know the principal Zapotec gods, among them Quetzalcoatl, god of wind; Xipe, god of springtime and patron of jewellers; *Ill. 67* Xochipilli, god of flowers and song; the goddess 13 Serpent; Cocijo, god of rain, and the companion gods. The polytheistic religion they represented was organized by a hierarchy with the Huijatoo or High Priest at its head.

It was during this period too that the architecture of Monte Albán reached its peak, the ground being levelled wherever necessary to erect its complex structures. The ball-court was built, as well as temple bases decorated with panels having two superimposed bands, sunken patios with altars in the middle, and buildings with columns. Houses built of stone were occupied by the aristocracy, while the common people lived on adjoining lands, lodged in houses or huts made of perishable materials.

The cult of the dead assumed a more complex character in this period: the tombs in which rulers and priests were buried comprised a staircase, antechamber, and funeral chamber, with niches along the inner walls and urns placed in the front of the façade; this was sometimes adorned with mural paintings. A reconstruction of Tomb 104 from Monte Albán shows these architectural features. A panel with two superimposed bands in the Monte Albán style adorns the façade, and a niche in the central section contains an urn of the Young God who wears the head-dress of Cocijo, god of rain. Within the chamber, which is rectangular and has a flat ceiling, can be seen the fresco paintings which decorate its walls. Prominent on the wall to the left is the figure of a priest holding a bag of copal in one hand – a symbolic gesture associated with the deity Xipe Totec – as well as a large yellow bird and a serpent with open jaws, both resting on a kind of box.

On the back wall appears the head of the God with a Bow in his Head-dress and the hieroglyph '5 Turquoise'; on the right-hand wall is a figure wearing a plumed serpent head-dress and a snake mask, associated with Quetzalcoatl. The skeleton of a person buried in an extended position lies on the ground with funerary offerings surrounding it and in the niches, just as when first excavated.

Between the years 800 and 1200 Zapotec culture declined, due largely to the penetration of Mixtecs who descended from near-by hills and mountains to conquer various Zapotec centres, such as Yagul, Teotitlán, and Monte Albán. Important dominions were subsequently founded – Teozacoalco, Tilan-tongo, Coixtlahuaca, Yanhuitlán, Tututepec, Mitla, and others – where Mixtec culture flourished.

In the section devoted to the Mixtecs are displayed replicas of their codices, which were made of deer skin and took the form of long strips folded like accordions and were painted in a wide range of colours. These constitute one of the salient features of this group and represent an exceptional pictorial tradition. Among them are the Selden, Nuttall, Bodley, Vindobonensis, and Colombino Codices, which record genea-logies, historic events, calendrical and religious themes, and conquests.

The artistic style of the Mixtecs is well exemplified in the adornment of the façades of their buildings. To the Zapotec use of a panel with two superimposed bands they added stone mosaics in which the geometric design projects from the back-ground. These were made of small stones, cut and assembled with precision, as seen at Mitla, Teotitlán, Yagul, and other sites. Their well-developed aesthetic sense is also evident in the pottery, which is characterized by its attractive colours and graceful shapes.

Wonderful specimens of ceramic work are on display, mainly polychrome vessels in shiny or matte finish and bearing

Ill. 72

Ill. 71

motifs of frets, flowers, human shin-bones, skulls, hieroglyphs, and gods, similar in style to the codices. Among the more noteworthy exhibits are pitchers with handles, tripod vases and jars, large earthen jars for funerary use, incense-burners with handles, vases with models of skeletons associated with the god of death, goblets, and zoomorphic vessels representing birds and deer.

Another craft in which the Mixtecs excelled was metalworking; they employed techniques of hammering, soldering, *cire-perdue* (lost-wax) casting, gilding, and filigree, mainly for working gold, silver, and copper. By these means they produced laminated bracelets, repoussé disks, ear-plugs, pectorals, nose-plugs, bead necklaces, rings, bells, pendants, handles for fans, needles, and many other articles, out of a highly creative imagination.

In the Oaxaca Room there is a partial reconstruction of the contents of Tomb 7 at Monte Albán, in which nine skeletons were found, accompanied by remarkable grave goods. The Mixtec objects include delicate jewellery such as rings with pendant ornaments, composite pectorals, bracelets, pendants, necklaces, pearls, and bone objects.

Ill. 74

Outstanding pieces of jewellery are the famous pectoral from Yanhuitlán, which is in the shape of a shield crossed by a sheaf of arrows worked in gold with a mosaic of turquoise; the pectoral from Zaachila with a large bell upon which the figure of a human being or a god appears to be seated; and another extraordinary pectoral from Oaxaca depicting the god Xiuhtecuhtli, who is associated with fire.

The Mixtecs were highly skilled in the working of semiprecious stones; from onyx and alabaster they made vases of elegant forms, usually with supports; from rock-crystal they fashioned beads for necklaces, lip-plugs, and skulls; jade was shaped into plaques with engraved figures of gods (*penates*). They also worked in wood, from which they carved masks covered with turquoise and shell mosaics, drums, spearthrowers beautifully ornamented in low relief, and handles for sacrificial knives. Choice examples of all these are exhibited.

Bone too was used, for carving tablets with calendrical and religious motifs in low relief – comparable to the ivory miniatures of Old World cultures.

To sum up, the Zapotecs were great potters, architects, astronomers, and mathematicians, intellectually advanced and with a profound feeling for religion, while the Mixtecs were great painters of codices, ceramists, lapidaries, and gold- and silversmiths, whose meticulous works of art were the expression of an acute sensibility.

61 *(left, above)* Mask representing the bat god. Stone. Zapotec. Height: 19 cm. Protoclassic. Monte Albán II

62 *(above)* Brazier with Olmec face. Clay. Zapotec. Height: 17 cm. Upper Preclassic. Monte Albán I

63 *(left)* Vessel with human figure and long spout on opposite sides. Clay. Zapotec. Height: 23 cm. Upper Preclassic. Monte Albán I

64 *(right)* Jaguar with necklace, decorated with fresco painting. Clay. Zapotec. Height: 85 cm. Protoclassic. Monte Albán II

65 *(left)* Model of pillared temple containing a parrot, associated with the Sun. Clay. Zapotec. Height: 34 cm. Protoclassic. Monte Albán II

66 *(right)* Pair of figures known as 'Xantiles', which are lids for braziers with attributes of gods. Clay. Mixtec. Height: 39 and 42 cm. Postclassic. Monte Albán IV

67 *(right)* Urn in the form of a goddess. Clay. Zapotec. Height: 25 cm. Classic. Monte Albán IIIA

68 *(right, centre)* The god Xipe Totec, 'our lord the flayed one', patron of springtime and jewellers. Clay. Zapotec. Height: 51 cm. Classic. Monte Albán IIIB

69 *(far right, below)* Figure of woman wearing twisted shawl as head covering, skirt and *quechquemitl*. Clay. Zapotec. Height: 34 cm. Classic. Monte Albán IIIB

70 Polychrome goblet with humming-bird on rim. Clay. Mixtec. Height: 7 cm. Postclassic. Monte Albán V

71 Tripod vase with Mictlantecuhtli, god of death attached. Clay. Mixtec. Height: 32 cm. Postclassic. Monte Albán V

72 (*right*) Polychrome tripod vase with codex-type decoration. Clay. Mixtec. Height: 15 cm. Postclassic. Monte Albán V

107

73 Polychrome vase representing the head of a deer. Clay. Mixtec. Height: 10 cm. Postclassic. Monte Albán V

74 Gold pectoral from Zaachila, gold and turquoise pectoral from Yanhuitlán, and gold pectoral with figure of the god Xiuhtecuhtli. Mixtec. Height: 10, Postclassic. Monte Albán V

The Gulf Coast Cultures

The region of the Gulf Coast extending from the Soto La Marina River in Tamaulipas to the Grijalva River in Tabasco saw the development of a series of cultures that can be separated into zones. The Olmecs lived in the north of Tabasco and the south of Veracruz; the Remojadas and Totonac peoples occupied Central Veracruz; and the Huastecs settled principally in the north of Veracruz and Tamaulipas. This hall is therefore divided into three corresponding sections.

By way of introduction the visitor is shown a statue or stela from Castillo de Teayo depicting the god Quetzalcoatl wearing *Ill. 75* a handsome pectoral in the shape of a sectioned conch shell as symbol of the wind, which we have come to associate with the Huastec culture. Next is a photo-mural of one of the panels that decorate the ball-court at El Tajín, typifying the cultures of Central Veracruz. The statue known as 'The Wrestler' is in *Ill. 77* characteristic Olmec style.

The section that follows, devoted to Olmec culture as a whole, starts with some fine stone statues including the Alvarado Stela, which shows a figure in profile facing a seated person whose hands are tied, evidently a captive; and the Izapa Tablet which has carved on it a ceremonial scene showing a beheaded ball-player and the priest who has performed the sacrifice.

In separate show-cases are to be seen a number of extra-ordinary Olmec sculptures of humans, both in clay and stone. These suggest that the Olmecs were usually of small stature with a tendency towards obesity, had slanting eyes, flat noses, and mouths with thick lips and turned-down corners, all of which makes them resemble new-born babies or gives them a *Ill. 76* feline appearance. There are evident signs of cranial defor- *Ill. 81* mation, as well as of head shaving and dental mutilation.

109

On display are examples of pottery, which was principally black, white, or grey, and variously decorated; the forms *Ill. 78* include dishes, vases with a flat bottom, gourd-shaped or narrow-necked bowls, and zoomorphic vessels of great beauty.

Stone-carving played an important role among the Olmecs, and their tools included chisels, hammers, awls, and drills made of hard stone, such as serpentine and quartz; abrasives of water and sand were used to obtain highly polished, shiny surfaces. Olmec lapidaries produced delicate ornaments and splendid statues and figurines, all carved in semi-precious stones, green-coloured ones being favoured. Among the exhibits are bead necklaces, plain or engraved ear-plugs, pectorals or plaques to be hung round the neck, pendants in the form of jaguar teeth, as well as mirrors carved from magnetite with a certain convexity which enlarges the image.

That the Olmecs had acquired knowledge of the calendar, of numeration, and hieroglyphic writing is evident from monuments at La Venta, Tres Zapotes, Cerro de las Mesas, and Monte Albán. By way of illustration there is a replica of the Tuxtla Statuette which represents a man with a duck-billed mask and bears the date A D 162; also Stela C from Tres Zapotes, Veracruz with the date 31 B C on one side and on the other a jaguar mask in low relief.

The art of the Olmecs found inspiration in the jaguar, treated both as a deity related to rain and as a totemic animal. It was *Ill. 82* customary for votive axes, masks and statues, plaques, figurines, and other objects to bear his image, as is shown by a number of *Ill. 80* the exhibits, for example, an axe with the face of the jaguar god. Other noteworthy objects include a carving of a human head from Tenango del Valle; models of hunchbacks, dwarfs, and other misshapen diseased beings, as well as delicate jade or serpentine figurines conveying the physical type of these people, although in somewhat idealized form.

Ill. 79 Our Olmec legacy includes human masks of great beauty, votive axes such as the one from Simojovel with a human face *Ill. 83* engraved on it, and a hollow jade canoe. The section concludes with a monolithic stone box with designs carved in low relief, a tablet from La Venta depicting a priest seated on a rattlesnake, and a colossal head from Tres Zapotes, Veracruz, placed on a slight rise in the garden outside the hall. *Ill. 84*

It is now established that Olmec culture originated and evolved somewhere south of Veracruz and north of Tabasco over a period extending from at least as far back as 1500 B C to the time of Christ. It was these people who laid the foundations on which civilization was built, and with justification they have been called the mother culture of Mesoamerica. Their most noteworthy accomplishments are their remarkable work in stone – an inspiration to later cultures – and the invention of the calendar, numeration, and hieroglyphic writing, which were subsequently further developed, mostly by the Maya.

The second section of this hall is devoted to the cultures that emerged and developed at diverse times in various parts of Central Veracruz, at places such as Alvarado, Nautla, Orizaba, and Papaloapan. Remojadas, Nopiloa, Cerro de las Mesas, Paso de Ovejas, El Tajín, and other Preclassic and Classic sites are represented, as well as the Isla de Sacrificios, Zempoala, Quiahuiztlan, and others of the Postclassic Totonac culture.

The first exhibit is a handsome clay statue representing the old god of fire – Huehueteotl – with a large brazier on his head. *Ill. 85* From the figures contained in a near-by sequence of show-cases it is evident that the people were of short stature, had straight hair and aquiline noses, that they practised cranial deformation, dental mutilation, and scarification on the chest and shoulders, and often blackened their teeth with tar and painted their hair and cheeks with the same substance; other figures again have shaven heads. They were fond of dressing in braids and showy head-dresses, decorative turbans with motifs of herons, scrolls, bows and frets, plumes, helmets with descending or stylized birds, and tall conical caps; items of clothing included the *quechquemitl*, short skirts, sashes, the *huipil*, loin-cloths, hats, and sandals. Personal appearance was enhanced by necklaces, nose-plugs, ear-plugs, bracelets, lip-plugs, and other ornaments.

There is a fine display of pottery from Central Veracruz,
Ill. 86 including various anthropomorphic vessels of the Remojadas
culture in which tar is used as decoration. Other exhibits include
Ill. 89 a handsome globular seed jar with a centipede painted in red
over orange, a vessel with the figure of an old man, another in
Ill. 87 the shape of an armadillo. Also lovely Smiling Head figurines,
mould-made figures from Nopiloa and Lirios, toys in the form
of little jaguars or dogs on wheels, and models of deer painted
with tar from Paso de Ovejas.

The polytheistic nature of religion in the zone can be advanced
from effigies of gods such as Tlaloc, Xipe, Huehueteotl,
Ill. 88 Mictlantecuhtli, Xilonen, Ehecatl, Xochiquetzal, Xochipilli,
many of whom were introduced during the period of Mexica
conquests. Sun, moon, wind, fire, and fertility were also objects
of worship. Festivals in homage to the gods were accompanied
by dances and music, pantomimes, and ball-games. One of the
dances was the famous *Danza de los Voladores*, which is performed to this day; it had a religious solar symbolism because
the four 'flying' dancers, dressed as eagles and suspended by
ropes, have to descend from a tall pole round which they
revolve thirteen times before touching the ground, thereby
symbolizing the cycle of fifty-two years.

During the Preclassic horizon the various groups lived in
rural villages, inhabiting huts built upon platforms; as time went
on they began to build temple bases, ball-courts, palaces, etc.,
and so important centres or cities of a ceremonial character
arose. Among the more arresting buildings at El Tajín are the
pyramid known as Los Nichos (The Niches) on account of the
many niches that run all round the diminishing tiers, and a
ball-court adorned with panels carved in low relief and showing scenes related to this sport. A model of the ceremonial
centre of Tajín illustrates the appearance of towns and architecture in Central Veracruz.

The next exhibits are choice examples of the sculpture and
lapidary work of this zone; these include the Tablet of Huilo-
cintla on which a priest beautifully tattooed is shown piercing

his tongue with a stick – a form of auto-sacrifice – and the Tablet
of Tepetlaxco depicting a player attired in a wide belt to protect   *Ill. 90*
the stomach, knee-guards, and other clothing needed for the
ball-game. Also related to this game are handsome *yugos* (yokes)
carved in stone which were funerary replicas of the protective
belts; *palmas*, which seem to represent in stone a kind of plastron
or breastplate that was worn over the chest and held in place by
a belt; and votive *hachas* (axes) usually in the shape of human or
animal heads, which have perhaps some connection with the
beheading of players who lost. These are here exemplified by a
yoke in the form of a frog or feline animal and another in the   *Ill. 92*
shape of an owl; *palmas*, one anthropomorphic, another in the   *Ill. 91*
shape of an alligator, and a third depicting two hands placed
side by side; and various *hachas*, one of them showing a human
head wearing a dolphin head-dress.   *Ill. 94*

Towards the end of the Classic horizon the Totonacs began
to spread over the area from the mountains of Puebla to the
Gulf Coast; in their path they occupied sites such as Papantla,
Misantla, Isla de Sacrificios, Quiahuiztlan, Zempoala, and
Cerro Montoso, which they were still occupying on the arrival
of the Spaniards early in the sixteenth century.

Various pieces of pottery of theirs are on display – characteristically painted ware in red and brown over cream, or in an
orange colour with panels of gods and hieroglyphs – as well as
some alabaster vases with carvings of monkeys and other   *Ill. 93*
animals executed with great precision and skill.

Another exhibit is a model of the ceremonial centre of
Zempoala, noted for such buildings as the so-called 'Templo
Mayor', Temple of the Chimneys, and Temple of Quetzalcoatl. All these have stairways with low balustrades, whose
initial steep slant becomes almost vertical towards the top,
giving the structure the cube-like appearance characteristic of
Totonac architecture.

The last section is devoted to the Huastec culture, which
occupied the territory from the Soto La Marina River in
Tamaulipas to the Cazones River in Veracruz, with infiltrations

into San Luis Potosí and Querétaro. The neighbouring Totonacs influenced the culture of the Huastecs, and *vice versa*.

Ill. 95, 96

The visitor is first introduced to the statue known as the 'Huastec Adolescent'. Found on a ranch called El Consuelo on the outskirts of El Tamuin, San Luis Potosí, it portrays a young priest of the god Quetzalcoatl, or perhaps the god himself, since he carries on his back a child symbolizing the sun. His body is wonderfully tattooed with motifs of flowers, blades of corn, suns, heads of lizards, and other signs or hieroglyphs. He wears ear-plugs and the fingers of his right hand form a hollow, perhaps for inserting an offering.

Ill. 97

Some further Huastec figurines show that these people were well built with muscular legs and narrow waists, and had artificially deformed heads. They wore little clothing, painted their hair and their bodies, shaved the head or left individual locks of hair, had themselves tattooed, and used nose- and ear-plugs.

Sahagún tells us that the Huastecs häd flat heads and pierced their noses to insert tubular nose-plugs, to the ends of which they fixed plumes; he adds that they filed their teeth into points or dyed them black, painted their hair yellow or red, and wore feather haloes on their heads, disks of plumes on their backs, knee-length socks made of feathers, and bracelets on their arms.

Ill. 98
cf. Ill. 57
Ills. 99, 100

That the Huastecs were able potters is evident from the ceramic ware here exhibited: effigy vessels with spouts, vessels in the form of baskets with ribbon handles, anthropomorphic jars, and zoomorphic and phytomorphic vessels, all in a cream or white colour with motifs painted in dark red, black, orange, and dark brown.

Ill. 101

Another craft in which this group excelled was the carving of marine conch and other shells, from which they fashioned rings, ear-plugs, pectorals cut in spirals to symbolize the wind or beautifully sculptured in low relief, beads for necklaces in the form of skulls, plaques for sewing to their clothing, and many other objects. They also carved bone, wood, obsidian, jade, and other semi-precious stones.

The sculpture is in a style peculiar to the Huastecs and reveals aspects of their religion; most of it represents gods such as Quetzalcoatl, Tlazolteotl, Xilonen, Xipe, Tlaloc, Mictlante-cuhtli, and Xochiquetzal, of which the first two were the most important. Quetzalcoatl is usually shown wearing a conical *Ill. 102* cap, hook-shaped ear-plugs, and a pectoral made of a sectioned snail; Tlazolteotl, who carries a spindle and spindle whorl, wears a band of unspun cotton, a black streak on her mouth, and a tubular nose-plug.

These two gods were adopted into the Aztec pantheon and venerated in a special way, Tlazolteotl in particular. Historic sources tell us that the feast of this deity was celebrated in the month Ochpaniztli, in harvest-time, when Huastec servants, carrying huge phallic symbols bore the goddess in procession.

A statue from Ajalpan represents a young man dressed in an apron loin-cloth; others portray the god Mictlantecuhtli, god of death, and Xilonen, goddess of corn, dressed in a *quech-quemitl* and paper head-dress with a bow and decorated with ears of corn. A male figure wears a conical cap and turban adorned with a skull. All are indicative of the Huastec style in which the figure of a female earth goddess with arms crossed over her breast and wearing a head-dress or halo on the back of her head is dominant, but male figures with conical caps and clothing – sometimes showing the concept of life on one side and that of death on the other – also appear.

The Huastecs, in short, were good sculptors and lapidaries, and were skilled in carving shells; erected circular buildings over mounds or earth foundations; developed a handsome polychrome pottery; made a name for themselves as magicians or visionaries; and excelled in weaving blankets and stuffs. Today still they perpetuate certain customs, beliefs, and a language which have their origins in prehispanic times.

75 *(left)* Stela representing the god Quetzalcoatl as lord of the wind. He wears a pectoral of conch–shell sections and a conical cap. Stone. Huastec. Height: 3.07 m. Early Postclassic

76 *(right)* Figurine with features of child, a type referred to as 'baby face'. Clay. Olmec. Height: 18 cm. Middle Preclassic

77 *(below)* 'The Wrestler'. Stone. Olmec. Height: 66 cm. Proto-classic

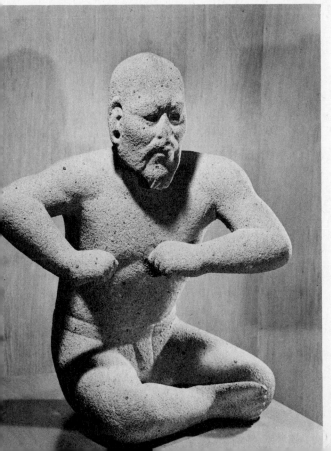

78 Flaring vase with globular base, decorated with designs in relief. Clay. Olmec. Height: 20 cm. Upper Preclassic

79 Mask with the mouth of a feline or of a new-born baby. Stone. Olmec. Height: 10 cm. Upper Preclassic

118

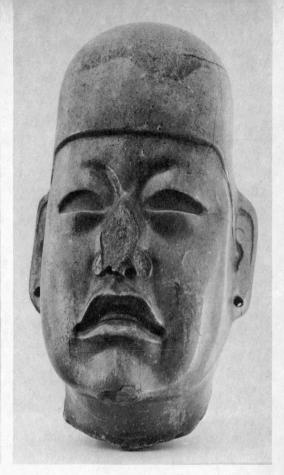

80 Ceremonial axe representing a child-jaguar deity, associated with rain. Stone. Olmec. Height: 22 cm. Upper Preclassic

81 Head showing cranial deformation, and characterized by the jaguar mouth. Stone. Olmec. Height: 19 cm. Protoclassic

82 Figure related to the jaguar cult, with deformed shaven head. Stone. Olmec. Height: 18 cm. Upper Preclassic

84 *(right)* Colossal head from Tres Zapotes. It is deformed and shaven and there are indications of a turban on the forehead. Stone. Olmec. Height: 2.27 m. Upper Preclassic

83 Model of canoe with incised designs. Stone. Olmec. Length: 20 cm. Upper Preclassic

85 Representation of Huehueteotl, old god of fire, with brazier on his head. Clay. Central Veracruz. Height: 84 cm. Classic

86 Anthropomorphic vessel with spout, painted with tar. Clay. Central Veracruz. Height: 27 cm. Middle Preclassic

87 *(right, above)* Smiling figurine. Clay. Central Veracruz. Height: 28 cm. Classic

88 *(far right, above)* Mictlantecuhtli, god of death. Clay. Central Veracruz. Height: 26 cm. Late Classic

89 *(right)* Vessel decorated with a centipede. Clay. Central Veracruz. Height: 15 cm. Late Classic

90 *(far left)* Tablet showing a priest performing auto-sacrifice. Related to the god Quetzalcoatl. Stone. Huastec influence. Height: 2.00 m. Late Classic

91 Palmate stone in the form of a human figure in profile. Stone. Central Veracruz. Height: 58 cm. Classic

92 Yoke representing monster of the earth and of death. Stone. Central Veracruz. Length: 41 cm. Classic

93 *(left)* Vase shaped in part like a monkey (cf. pl. 52). Alabaster. Central Veracruz. Height: 23 cm. Postclassic

94 Votive *hacha* in the shape of a human head with dolphin head-dress. Stone. Central Veracruz. Height: 28 cm. Classic

95, 96 *(left)* The 'Huastec Adolescent.' Believed to represent a young priest of the god Quetzalcoatl. Stone. Huastec. Height: 1.17 m. Late Classic

97 Woman wearing turban. Clay. Huastec. Height: 33 cm. Classic

98 Spouted polychrome vessel with human face on the neck. Clay. Huastec. Height: 29 cm. Postclassic

99 *(right, above)* Anthropomorphic vessel with spout. Clay. Huastec. Height: 20 cm. Postclassic

100 *(right)* Vessel in the shape of a monkey-like creature. Clay. Huastec. Height: 18 cm. Postclassic

128

101 Pectoral with relief showing
people and a plumed serpent.
Shell. Huastec. Height: 16 cm.
Postclassic

102 Deity related to death,
wearing a high conical cap and
hook-shaped ear-plugs. Stone.
Huastec. Height: 1.40 m.
Postclassic

The Maya

Let them not fall in climbing
Or descending the slopes,
Let no obstacle beset their path
To the fore or from behind;
Let them suffer no evil.
Grant them a good journey
Over beautiful smooth roads.

Popol Vuh

The territory occupied by the Maya stretches from the Grijalva River in Tabasco to the Ulua Valley in Honduras and the Lempa River in El Salvador. That is to say, it includes parts of Tabasco, Chiapas, Campeche, Yucatán, and Quintana Roo in Mexico, as well as Guatemala, Honduras, El Salvador, and Belice, British Honduras in Central America.

Physiographically and ecologically the Maya region can be divided into three large zones. The northern zone is a semi-arid plain embracing the Yucatán Peninsula, the maize fields of Campeche, and part of Quintana Roo, where such cities as Uxmal, Chichen Itzá, Kabáh, Labná, Mayapán, Edzná, Hochob, Cobá, and Tulúm were located. The central zone, predominantly humid tropical forest intersected by numerous rivers, reaches from Tabasco to Honduras, and here the ceremonial centres of Palenque, Bonampak, Yaxchilán, Calakmul, Uaxactún, Tikal, and Piedras Negras once flourished. The southern zone takes in the Highlands of Chiapas and Guatemala, where sites such as Chinkultic, Toniná, Kaminaljuyú, Chamá, Nebaj, and Zaculeu prospered.

All this is clearly shown in a large map just inside the entrance to this hall. In addition, the various' topographical features of the region are illustrated by means of colour photographs. There is also a diagram of the terrain in the form of an ideal cross-section running from the highlands to the coastal plains, and showing the changing vegetation encountered.

The physical aspect of the Maya and the clothing they wore are evident from stelae and Jaina figurines, as well as from photographs. These also illustrate certain customs practised by the Maya with the purpose of beautifying or distinguishing them from other peoples: cranial deformation, dental mutilation, tattooing or scarification, body painting, and induced cross-eyes. Other features which can still be observed in the Maya of today are pointed out, such as short stature, wide heads, dark skin, aquiline noses, high cheek-bones, slanting eyes with epicanthic fold, and the mongolian spot.

Where clothing and adornment are concerned, the clay figurines from Jaina run the gamut from the simple breech-clout of the common people to the rich garments and elaborate attire of the lords, priests, and women of high status. They enable the visitor to examine the exact nature of skirts, blouses, mantles or capes, sandals, belts, fans, animal helmets, hats, staffs of office, as well as of pectorals, bracelets, necklaces, ear-plugs, and other ornaments which reflect the rank and occupation of the individual in question.

Ill. 105 There are figurines showing lords and noblemen seated on their thrones or benches; priests and priestesses, usually carrying bags of incense; ball-players, warriors, musicians, weavers, and many other types. This indicates that Maya society was organized into well-defined classes or castes, with specialized activities. It is evident that there were two estates: the higher, formed of people in charge of the government, the priesthood, justice, and public administration; and the lower, composed of artisans, farmers, and the common people.

The practice of placing stelae and altars in front of pyramidal bases or buildings was a distinctive feature of the Maya culture. Its antecedents date back to the Protoclassic period from 200 B C to A D 200, when there was already this association of stela and altar at such sites as that of Izapa, Chiapas. Carved on Stela 1 from Izapa is a figure standing above a stream, wearing a kind of mask with serpent-like features and carrying a net, while the altar takes the form of a mythological animal – something between a jaguar and a frog – which is either crouching or ready to spring.

A show-case containing clay figurines and musical instruments gives some idea of the religious festivities of the Maya. In this regard it should be mentioned that music played quite an important role in their lives; there are flutes, whistles, ocarinas, rattles, drums, conch-shell trumpets, turtle-carapace drums, and other instruments, for the encouragement of the dancers, who wore masked costume. Among the other types of entertainment was the ball-game, which was played by the nobility and professional players.

Ritual feasts were governed by the religious calendar and were in honour of the gods, who had specific functions. For example, the Maya believed in a god, Hunab Kú, who was creator of all things; he in turn was father of Itzamná, god of the heavens and day and night. They also worshipped Kukulkán, god of wind; Chac, god of rain; Yum Kaax, young god of corn; Ek Chuah, patron of merchants; Ix Tab, god of suicides; Ix Chel, the moon goddess; Ah Puch, god of death, Ix Asal Uo, patroness of weaving, among others.

According to the Maya, the universe was divided into thirteen superior heavens where the Oxlahuntikú resided, and nine inferior heavens inhabited by the Bolontijú. The world was supported by the four Bacabs, related to the cardinal points, to four colours, and to four Chaques and four Iques, who helped the gods of rain and wind respectively. They also worshipped the great *ceiba*, sacred tree of life which sent its roots down into the earth, penetrating the world of death, and reached upward towards the thirteen superior heavens.

In this same section of the hall various stelae, lintels, hieroglyphs in stucco, and reproductions from the Tro-Cortesian Codex are exhibited; they underline the intellectual feats

133

achieved by the ancient Maya, who can claim to have been the scholars and mathematicians of the New World by virtue of their astronomical observations, knowledge of the calendar, mathematics, and hieroglyphic writing.

The Maya used a vigesimal system based on position, which led to their inventing zero. They wrote the numbers 1 to 19 by means of dots and bars, while zero was represented by a sort of shell. With these elements they could set down figures of almost any magnitude, placing the numerals in a horizontally ascending order; each successive position implied multiplying by 20, 400, 8000, etc. In their inscriptions they also used heads or figures as numerical symbols; stelae, lintels, staircases, and so on show that these were applied also to the calendar.

The religious calendar was composed of 20 day-names which were combined with 13 numbers to form a cycle of 260 days. The days were expressed in hieroglyphs and bore the names of Imix, Ik, Akbal, Kán, Chicchán, Cimi, Manik, Lamat, Muluc, Oc, Chuen, Eb, Ben, Ix, Men, Cib, Caban, Eznab, Cauac, and Ahau. The solar calendar was made up of 18 months of 20 days each, plus 5 additional days called Uayeb, making 365 days. The names of the months were Pop, Uo, Zip, Zotz, Tzec, Xul, Yaxkin, Mol, Chén, Yax, Zac, Ceh, Mac, Kankín, Muan, Pax, Kayab, Cumhú, and the Uayeb.

These two calendars were combined to form the 'Calendar Round' or cycle of 52 years, the minimum time in which any one date could be repeated. That is to say, if the religious calendar began with the day 1 Imix and the solar calendar with the month 0 Pop, the date 1 Imix 0 Pop could only recur after 18,980 days or 52 years had elapsed. The absolute date was fixed in Maya terms by counting from a legendary year the significance of which we have no means of assessing. This method of reckoning is known as the 'Long Count' and was expressed in Baktuns, Katuns, Tuns, Uinals, and Kins – units of time, as recorded on the stelae.

Besides a precise solar or civil calendar – allowing for the fraction of time left over and the leap years – the Maya calculated the length of the lunar cycles, the seasons, the equinoxes and solstices, and the Venus cycle of 584 days, as well as making observations about other planets and constellations. They also left tablets on which the predicted dates of future eclipses were recorded, as can be seen in the Dresden Codex. Their hieroglyphic writing, which has not yet been completely deciphered, was also a great aid to learning.

Prominence is given to the evolution of pottery, the changing shapes and types of which correspond to the successive phases. Thus the pottery of the Early Preclassic phase (1300–800 BC) is distinguished by all-over colouring in cream, red, orange, or black, with white rims. The shapes include jars marked in sections like a squash, composite-profile vessels, dishes with flat base, goblets with ring base, and jars with simple spout.

The next phase of the Preclassic, known as the Chicanel and lasting from 800 to 200 BC, produced vessels in two colours, such as black on red, red on brown, red on white, and orange on cream. The forms resemble those of the previous phase. There follows the Matzanel or Protoclassic period (200 BC–AD 200) in which ceramic elements highly characteristic of the Maya are introduced, such as tetrapod vessels, mammiform supports, spool pot-stands, painted decoration over dry stucco, *Ill. 106* labial and basal flanges, spouts connected by a bridge, and other variations usually applied to polychrome ware.

During the flowering of Maya culture in the Classic period (AD 200–900), polychrome decoration predominates, first on vessels embellished with geometric or animal motifs, and later on vases which resemble codices in that they depict ceremonies, hunts, scenes of war, and other subjects. At this time slate-coloured ware was being made in the Yucatán Peninsula and *Ills. 103, 117* *Ill. 104* some Teotihuacán influence can be seen in the pottery.

The Postclassic (AD 900–1519) represents a decadent stage in ceramics, since there is a return to a domestic type of pottery and to the representation of figures of gods and priests, especially on *Ills. 107, 119* urns and braziers which are sometimes painted in colours mixed with water. However, there was also a certain commercial interchange with other regions, as the presence of Fine Orange and 'plumbate' ware shows.

From Maya ceramics the visitor passes on to the architecture and sculpture characteristic of ceremonial centres at the peak of their development in the Classic period. There are photo-murals of Structure E-VII-Sub at Uaxactún and of one of the temples at Tikal, illustrating the style of the first pyramidal bases in this region; these, besides being stepped, have receding and protruding apron mouldings at the corners.

Also on display are models of such ceremonial centres as Piedras Negras, in the Guatemalan part of the Usumacinta Valley, which uses to good advantage natural irregularities of the terrain; and Copán, Honduras. The latter centre is distinguished for its temple bases with tiers having vertical walls, and their wide staircases, some of which are adorned with hundreds of hieroglyphs; its large statues and stelae, its ball-courts, altars, and other civil and ceremonial structures. Attention is drawn to the architectural style of temples – whose inspiration was the Maya hut. The discovery of the false arch or corbelled vault topped with capstones and the use of roof crests over the temples were the most important contributions of Maya architecture.

Ills. 108, 109
Ill. 116
Ill. 111
Maya sculpture is represented by beautiful lintels and stelae from Yaxchilán, a statue from Toniná, the Jonuta Tablet, a disk from Chinkultic, stelae from Calakmul, and other excellent examples. Of particular interest is the panel of the Foliated Cross from Palenque in which two priests – shown in profile – make offerings to a deified corn plant which takes the form of a cross; carved in the upper section is a quetzal.

Ill. 110
Ill. 112
The skill and aesthetic refinement of the Maya craftsmen manifests itself also in minor arts. To show how delicately they worked bone and jade, for example, the exhibits include a jaguar's bone, carved in the shape of a priest, several examples of pectorals or plaques fashioned in jade and serpentine, a small tablet from Palenque showing Chac, god of rain, and beads for necklaces and ear-plugs, all exquisitely carved.

A stairway leads down to the section of the hall devoted to burials and funerary practices. Direct burial in the ground accompanied by offerings, burial in large earthenware jars, and finally a full-size replica of the burial chamber at Palenque show the progression from the simplest to the most complex.

This leads on naturally to a model of the ceremonial centre of Palenque with its group of temples and buildings erected upon pyramidal bases; here are to be seen the Temple of the Sun, the Temple of the Foliated Cross, the Palace, the Temple of the Count, the Aqueduct, and, of particular interest, the Temple of the Inscriptions, where an interior chamber was found containing the sarcophagus of one of the rulers of the site.

Near by are the jewels which accompanied the occupant of the tomb: two masks worked in a jade mosaic, necklaces of the *Ill. 115* same material, rings, ear-plugs, pearls, and brooches, or objects to hang from the belt. Also on view are heads modelled in stucco which were found with the stone sarcophagus, and a *Ill. 114* full-scale reconstruction of the royal chamber, with the tablet, sarcophagus, and burial of the deceased, just as it was found in the archaeological excavation.

Returning to ground level the visitor passes on to objects of the Postclassic horizon in which Central Mexican influence is frequently seen; this influence reached as far as the Puuc or mountain cities in the Yucatán Peninsula. Among the pieces of sculpture they yielded are the head of a ruler with tattooing on *Ill. 118* his cheek, and a mask of Chac, the rain god, worked in stone mosaic, both from Kabáh; and the sculpture known as the 'Queen of Uxmal', which actually portrays a young priest inside the jaws of a serpent, related to the god Kukulkán. *Ill. 120*

The atlantes of Chichen Itzá take the form of sculptured *Ill. 122* warriors dressed in feather capes, short skirts, pectorals, ear-plugs, and sandals; there too a characteristic Chac-Mool was found outside the Temple of the Warriors. Minor sculptures from various other sites of the Yucatán Peninsula also show Central Mexican influence.

The architecture of this period is represented by a model of

137

the Castillo at Chichen Itzá, a structure comprising a pyramidal base with nine tiers, on each side of which is a great stairway whose low balustrades are shaped like serpents: their heads are at the bottom and their bodies ascend to form serpentine columns for the temple. There is too a model of the walled ceremonial sanctuary of Tulúm on the shores of the Caribbean Sea – showing such impressive buildings as the Palace, the Temple of the Descending God, and the Temple of the Frescoes – whose paintings have a certain Mixtec flavour.

Among the objects in the show-cases are: examples of 'plumbate' ware; animals or vases carved in onyx or alabaster; Fine Orange vessels with decorated panels; disks with a mosaic *Ill. 113* overlay of turquoise, shell, and pyrite found in the substructure *Ill. 121* of the Castillo at Chichen Itzá; and eccentric flint axes which were part of the staffs of office carried by the nobility.

Metalworking was introduced into the Maya region through trade with Central America, principally from Costa Rica and Panama. Among the gold objects on display are figurines, bells, repoussé disks, small containers, and other items recovered from the Sacred Cenote of Chichen Itzá, where the Maya made sacrifices and offerings to the water god.

In the garden outside this hall the following are to be seen: replicas of stelae from Quirigúa, Piedras Negras, and Copán; a scale model of a building at Hochob, Campeche, whose façade is in the typical Chenes style with a large mask of the rain god framing the doorway; and a replica of the Temple of Paintings at Bonampak, with its three rooms decorated with frescoes. On the walls of the first of these rooms is painted a scene showing a retinue of lords and nobles at the ceremonial presentation of the heir to the throne of Bonampak. Several richly attired priests are in attendance, and the celebration ends with a dance accompanied by musicians playing drums made of turtle carapaces or with leather drum-heads, rattles, and large trumpets. The dancers are disguised as crabs and alligators, or wear masks adorned with plant motifs.

In the second room is to be seen a battle, full of action and colour, bristling with spears and shields, trophy heads, animal masks, and painted warriors. Another scene shows the trial and punishment of the prisoners by the chief of Bonampak, who wears a jaguar skin vest and sandals and carries in his hand a royal lance.

The frescoes on the walls of the third room extol the victory won by Bonampak – great celebrations being held in the open and on the steps of a principal building. Taking part are dancers wearing quetzal-feather head-dresses and short skirts – movement is indicated by the billowing skirts – acrobats, musicians, and a retinue of lords and nobles including the royal family and heir to the throne.

The civilization of the Maya, culturally refined and distinguished by a singular aptitude for the arts and crafts and by a high degree of scholarship, was still flourishing at the time of the Spanish Conquest of Mexico in 1519.

103 Vase in form of
jaguar-head. Clay. Height:
23 cm. Late Classic. Tepeu

104 *(right, above)* Vase of
'Yucatecan Slate' type.
Clay. Height: 12 cm. Late
Classic. Puuc period

105 Important personage
seated on a throne or
circular bench. Clay.
Height: 22 cm. Classic

106 Dish with basal
moulding and mam-
miform supports. Clay.
Height: 14 cm. Early
Classic. Tzakol

107 Polychrome plate
showing a person of
importance, surrounded
by a band of
hieroglyphs. Clay.
Diameter: 35 cm.
Late Classic. Tepeu

108 *(left)* Stela 10 of Yaxchilán, Chiapas. Stone. Height: 1.93 m. Late Classic. AD 766

109 Lintel 53 from Yaxchilán, Chiapas. Stone. Height: 1.60 m. Late Classic

110 Illustrious personage wearing rich apparel. Bone. Height: 7 cm. Classic

111 (right) Plaque or pectoral in the form of a human figure in relief. Stone. Length: 9 cm. Classic

112 (below) Disk from Chinkultic, Chiapas, showing a ball-player. Stone. Diameter: 55 cm. Classic. AD 590

113 (right, below) Disk with mosaic of turquoise, shell and flint. Chichen Itzá, Yucatán. Diameter: 24 cm. Postclassic

114 Human head, modelled in
the typical Palenque style.
Stucco. Height: 28 cm. Classic

116 (*right*) Tablet from Jonuta,
Tabasco, showing a priest
making offerings to a cacao
plant. Stone. Height: 1.03 m.
Classic

115 Jade mask composed
of several parts. Stone. Height:
8 cm. Classic. Palenque, Chiapas

117 Polychrome vase showing a person of importance. Clay. Height: 13 cm. Late Classic

119 (*right*) Priest presenting offering of incense. Polychrome clay. Mayapán, Yucatán. Height: 56 cm. Postclassic

118 Fragment of sculpture known as the 'King of Kabáh'. The face is scarified. Stone. Height: 48 cm. Late Classic. Puuc period

120 Priest emerging from the jaws of a serpent. Associated with Kukulkán, civilizing god-hero. Stone. Height: 80 cm. Late Classic. Puuc period

122 (*right*) Atlante in the form of a warrior. Stone. Height: 88 cm. Postclassic. Toltec influence

121 Eccentric axe with human silhouettes. Flint. Height: 32 cm. Late Classic

The North of Mexico

In the northern border areas of Mesoamerica individual cultures also developed, although the peoples here came under influence of the advanced cultures of the Central Highlands and West Mexico, and still more of the United States Southwest. This hall is concerned with Guanajuato, San Luis Potosí, Zacatecas, Durango, and Chihuahua – those parts of what may be termed Marginal Mesoamerica where a sedentary life was possible.

Actually, owing to its diversity of climates and restricting ecological factors, the north of Mexico was shared by different groups at different times. Thus there were nomadic hunters of large Pleistocene mammals who reached the Central Highlands when climatic conditions were more favourable than they are today; groups of food-gatherers who lived in woody and even arid zones, similar to those who occupied the United States Southwest and are now known as Desert Cultures; groups who derived from these but who settled in the north-west of Mexico and practised riparian agriculture; and mobile groups of seasonal hunters and gatherers who made incursions into the sedentary sites having a higher cultural niveau, and who still subsisted at the time of the Spanish Conquest.

In order to make this plain, the first thing to be seen in this hall is a coloured map showing the cultural zones of North Mexico: those occupied by the Desert Culture and by the Plains Culture of Marginal Mesoamerica, and that of Oasis-America. A second map shows the progressive colonization of Northern Mexico by Spain and its effect on the groups living there at the time of the Conquest.

Artifacts of the Plains and Desert Cultures respectively are exhibited in separate show-cases, thus differentiating those of the hunters from those of the gatherers. Projectile points used by the Plains people in hunting mammoths, horses, bison, and other animals, on the one hand; nets, baskets, sandals, and wooden objects on the other. A third map shows the location of the principal sites at which such artifacts and other material of archaeological interest have been found. There are also reproductions of rock paintings.

Although the groups of the marginal zone have characteristics of their own, trade and interchange of ideas with Mesoamerica are apparent. This contact of the North with the South meant that what each produced in the way of pottery, weaving, architecture, and metalworking had much in common with the other.

Materials from Marginal Mesoamerica, as represented by the Guanajuato, San Luis Potosí, and Zacatecas groups, are next exhibited. There are examples of pottery from San Miguel Allende and El Cóporo characterized by vessels in brushed white *Ills.123,128* and red on brown with human-effigy brazier covers used for *Ill. 124* burning copal, clay pipes, polychrome vessels derived from the Chupícuaro type, shell ornaments, and other items. Among the objects from the several sites of San Luis Potosí are vessels painted black on red.

The Preclassic culture of Chupícuaro engendered other Guanajuato groups which gradually migrated towards Michoacán, Zacatecas, and Durango; Queréndaro, Lago de Cuitzeo, Suchil, Chalchihuites, and even La Quemada show this *Ill. 130* influence, as does the Hohokam culture, thus forming a corridor of reciprocal influences between Mesoamerica and the United States Southwest.

The section of the hall devoted to Zacatecas contains examples of pottery – the black type with cloisonné or scraped decoration and a red type on cream, using motifs of small animals such as scorpions, snakes, and squirrels is particularly arresting – decorated spindle whorls, metal objects, and other items in which contact with other groups is evident. A good idea of the architecture of this region, which employed adobe and stone slabs in its structures and combined Mesoamerican features with those of the United States Southwest can be obtained from photo-murals of La Quemada.

La Quemada is situated on the spurs of the Palomas mountain range, and the ceremonial centre – whose builders took advantage of the terrain and used walls up to 10 metres high on different levels – gives the appearance of a fortified city. A wide avenue can be seen leading to the centre proper, where stands a truncated pyramid with a steep staircase; surrounding it are structures with columns made of slabs, rooms around sunken patios, and pyramidal bases of small dimensions.

The section on Chihuahua is the most extensive and focuses on the culture of Casas Grandes in particular. Photo-murals show the principal features of this site: adobe houses of one or more storeys, similar to those of Mesa Verde and other places in the United States Southwest, and an oval ball-court; irrigation canals and cisterns for storage of water; ovens for cooking *mezcal*, mud cages for parakeets, and much besides.

The pottery produced by the people of Casas Grandes was very striking; something similar is still being made by the Pueblo, Pima, and Pápago Indians. Coloured black, dark red, and dark brown over cream or ivory, it takes the form of simple *Ill. 126* bowls and jars, with stylized animals or geometric drawings, or *Ill. 127* vessels with human and animal effigies.

On display too are objects made of shell, necklaces with *Ill. 125* turquoise and shell beads, a copper bell in the shape of a turtle *Ill. 129* made by casting and applied wire, grooved axes, and a number of other articles, many of them imported.

It took almost four hundred years to conquer and pacify the North, a process in which Spanish, French, British, and other nationals participated. This is largely explained by the fact that most of this region was inhabited by nomadic hunting-gathering groups who loved their liberty and tenaciously opposed subjugation. This aspect too receives visual elucidation by means of maps of the period and explanatory pictures.

123 Jar of 'brushed white' type. Clay. San Miguel Allende, Guanajuato. Height: 39 cm. Late Classic. (Private collection)

124 Brazier covers in the form of human busts. Clay. San Miguel Allende, Guanajuato. Height: 19 and 18 cm. Early Postclassic. (Private collection)

125 *(left)* Turquoise mosaic
pectoral from shell neck-
lace. Casas Grandes, Chi-
huahua. Height: 26 cm.
Postclassic

126 Polychrome vessel
with geometric
decoration. Clay. Casas
Grandes, Chihuahua.
Height: 19 cm. Postclassic

127 Polychrome
vessels with human faces
and geometric decoration.
Clay. Casas Grandes, Chi-
huahua. Height: 14 and
16.5 cm. Postclassic

128 Whistling vessel incorporating seated human figure. Clay. El Cóporo, Guanajuato. Height: 28 cm. Late Classic

129 Model turtle made by casting in a mould, then applying filigree. Copper. Casas Grandes, Chihuahua. Length: 10 cm. Postclassic

130 Polychrome jars of La Quemada style. Clay. Zacatecas. Height: 15 and 11 cm. Early Postclassic

Western Mexico

All the moons, all the years,
All the days and all the winds
Run their course and have an end.
All living creatures also reach
Their time of repose.
   Chilam Balam de Chumayel

The last of the halls is devoted to cultures that flourished in Sinaloa, Nayarit, Colima, Jalisco, Michoacán, and part of Guerrero and Guanajuato, thus covering a vast region of Western Mexico from the Guasave River to the Balsas Valley. Over a long period of time groups of settlers came here to occupy the littoral, the mountains and volcanic plateaux, the lake valleys and the broad plains; as a result a number of local cultures evolved which are distinguished for their unique and original works of art.

On entering, the visitor encounters a large map in colour, showing not only the topography, flora and fauna of the region, but some of the distinctive cultural achievements of these peoples. Thus Chupícuaro is characterized by its delightful little figurines and elegant pottery; Colima, Jalisco, and Nayarit are noted for their realistic and expressive clay figures; Mezcala excelled in stone-carving, Sinaloa in working shell; while the Tarascans developed feather-work and were skilled gold- and silversmiths.

A second map, in metal, illustrating the region's cultural evolution, shows that Western Mexico was a kind of channel through which influences from other cultures flowed at different periods. Thus the United States Southwest introduced grooved axes, clay and stone pipes, disks or mirrors with pyrite mosaics, bracelets of cut conch and other shells; while shaft-tombs, metallurgy, vessels with a stirrup spout, stone maces, effigy milling-stones, and much besides came by way of the Pacific from Central America. At the same time, Mesoamerica made its own cultural contributions northward and southward to those areas.

The earliest occupants of Western Mexico lived in rural villages, cultivating corn, beans, and squash. Their huts were made of perishable materials, they venerated their dead, and *Ill. 134* produced pottery and figurines of refined elegance such as those from El Opeño and Chupícuaro.

At this latter site the dead were inhumed usually close to the houses and accompanied by plentiful grave goods, as the collective burial here reproduced shows. Clay vessels, monochrome, dichrome, and polychrome, take many different forms: tripod dishes with tall supports, bowls shaped like a squash, vessels with basket handles, goblets, and containers with human faces near the rim. Black, red, and dark brown upon a cream or white background were mainly used for the polychrome ware.

The figurines from both Chupícuaro and El Opeño on display tell us much about these peoples. There are babies in cradles, musicians with flutes, men with merchandise on their backs, women with children, and so on. The great majority are *Ill. 132* flat in shape, and some of them are painted in blue and black; but a few larger figures, for which black and cream on red were used, are hollow.

During the Classic horizon the population increased and more sites in Western Mexico were settled; some of these grew into simple ceremonial centres where various crafts were developed and a theocratic government evolved. It was at this time that the cultures of Colima, Jalisco, and Nayarit flourished, each producing its own readily recognizable clay figurines and pottery.

The potters of Colima produced vessels mainly in polished red or brown ware; others simulate plants and fruits or are in

the shape of a human figure. There are models of fattened dogs, *Ill. 136*
squirrels, snakes, parrots, woodpeckers, crabs, chameleons, and
other animals, while some take the form of squashes held up by
supports shaped like dwarfs or birds, carriers of benches,
water-carriers, and women.

The Colima figurines, both solid and hollow, likewise reveal
many facets of the daily life of the people: chiefs seated on *Ill. 135*
benches or on litters, priests, dancers, musicians, warriors, and *Ill. 133*
water-carriers are among the characters represented, and their
clothing and adornments – loin-cloths, shirts or vests, trousers,
capes, chin-straps, helmets, *quechquemitls*, necklaces, and ear-
plugs – are easily recognizable. The non-figural pieces even give
us information about architecture, since there are models of
huts and temples set on pyramidal bases.

The potters of Nayarit specialized in the production of
hollow figures – many of them quite large – in a style approach-
ing caricature, for which they always used white, yellow, and
brown paint over the reddish or brownish clay. Worthy of
note are models of diseased or misshapen individuals, as well
as of men and women engaged in various activities. Their legs *Ill. 139*
and arms are usually disproportionate and they wear nose- and *Ill. 138*
ear-plugs made of a string of hoops or rings. In the same way the
solid figurines throw light on various aspects of the times, for
there are models of houses, ball-courts and players, groups of *Ill. 131*
dancers and musicians, and even burial scenes.

The figurines from Jalisco, finished in a burnished cream-
coloured clay, depict both men and women, and some show that
body painting was used. One of the most striking of these takes *Ill. 142*
the form of an old man who carries a cane walking-stick and *Ill. 137*
stands on a fish; in style it is reminiscent of Colima, whose
direct influence is evident.

The majority of the pieces from these three States represent
mortuary offerings found in shaft-tombs – vaulted funerary
chambers to which access was gained through a shaft or chimney
– similar to those found in Colombia and Ecuador in South
America. Among the exhibits is a replica of a tomb at Etzatlán.

Ills. 143, 140

The State of Guerrero is represented by many objects from Mezcala, whose special style of stone-carving is to be seen in models of temples, masks, axes with human figures in outline, plaques, and other ornaments, usually made of green stone. There are also examples of pottery decorated in a lacquered style using blue, green, pink, and yellow.

Next in order come the cultures that flourished during the Postclassic horizon, when there were many new developments such as the introduction of metallurgy, pipes and tobacco, the art of feather-working, the construction of *yácatas*, and the first written sources. Tribal wars were a feature of this time, which saw the emergence of the Guasave, Culiacan, Ixtlán groups and of the Tarascans of Michoacán.

Ill. 141

Now, too, the inhabitants of Sinaloa evolved the so-called Aztatlán Complex, whose impressive burial customs are a salient feature: the dead were wrapped in *petates* (reed mats) or blankets – which were bound with cords – and buried with numerous offerings, or they were placed in large earthen jars or urns. The Aztatlán Complex has yielded clay masks, grooved axes, pipes, shell bracelets, metal objects, mirrors in pyrite mosaic, gourds decorated in lacquer, vases carved in *tecali* or alabaster, and polychrome pottery in which areas of colour are outlined with incising.

The rest of the hall is devoted to the Tarascan culture which developed in Uayameo, Pátzcuaro, Tzintzuntzan, Ihuatzio, and many other sites that in time became dominions of importance. They spread over a vast territory, imposing their language and customs on other groups; that is to say, their society was imperialistic like that of their contemporaries the Mexicas.

The Tarascans cultivated a variety of plants, including tobacco, cotton and *chia* (flax seed), the last-named providing both a beverage and oil. In the lake regions they fished from canoes using nets, fish-hooks, harpoons, and spear-throwers. They used cotton as well as down produced by the *ceiba* tree, *maguey* fibres, rabbit fur, and feathers to make distinctive garments.

They were skilled potters, producing such things as stirrup- *Ill. 144*
spouted, shoe-shaped, and miniature vessels, bowls with sections like a pumpkin and with basket handles, polychrome
vessels with negative decoration, as well as clay pipes. They also
excelled in feather-work, using the feathers in mosaic form to
fashion shields, blankets, fans, figures, and other articles.

Striking examples of obsidian carving are on view, among
them highly polished mirrors, ear-plugs as delicate as glass –
sometimes embellished with turquoise and gold mosaics – and
lip-plugs; also various choice pieces of metalwork, principally
bells, rings, bracelets, tweezers, disks, pins, masks, and lip-
plugs. In working metals the Tarascans applied techniques of
cold-forging, casting in moulds or by the *cire-perdue* (lost-wax)
process, filigree work, soldering and gilding, using copper, gold, *Ill. 145*
and silver as well as alloys of these.

'Michoacán is the richest in metals of all New Spain – in
copper and tin as well as gold and silver,' wrote Motolinia in
the sixteenth century, and his statement is confirmed by the
existence of placer mines and gold-bearing sand pits in rivers
such as the Zacatula and Balsas; by deposits of gold, silver, and
copper at Motines del Oro, Ostutla, Morcillo, Pomaro, and
other sites; and by the so-called 'Canvas of Jucutacato', painted
in his day, which describes in pictorial form the movement of
people in search of mines across various parts of the Tarascan
kingdom.

This last section of the hall contains a mural devoted to the
religion of the Tarascans and to the semi-divine character of
the Cazonci, principal ruler of their kingdom. He personified
the god Curicaveri, god of fire, of the sun, and of the sky, and
was the only person whose body could be cremated when he
died.

Besides the god Curicaveri the Tarascans worshipped the
goddess Cueraváperi, creatress and mother of the gods;
Tariácuri, god of wind; Xaratanga, goddess of subsistence;
Uinturópati, goddess of corn, and other deities. They conceived
of the universe as being divided into three superposed realms,

each one with its four cardinal points, four special deities, and four distinctive colours.

Then there is a model of the ceremonial centre of Tzintzuntzan, which was the ancient capital of the Tarascan kingdom. It is located on the lower spurs of the Cerro Yahuarato facing Lake Patzcuaro within the purlieus of the present-day town of Tzintzuntzan.

This ceremonial centre comprises a large artificial terrace with stepped tiers adapted to natural irregularities of the terrain. Near the middle are remnants of a staircase which gave access to this terrace. Occupying this terrace, which is 400 metres wide at the front, are five temple bases or *yácatas*, so arranged as to juxtapose rectangular and circular floor plans in regular alignment. From the Relación (Chronicle) of Michoacán we know that on these circular bases stood round temples made of tree-trunks and straw.

Near by lay the great ceremonial Plaza flanked by dwellings for priests and nobles; the various districts also had their own *yácatas* arranged in the manner of main temples. Important persons were usually interred in front of the *yácatas*, and many burials with offerings have been found under the terrace floor; there were also holes which had been used for cremation.

Ill. 147

The final exhibits are of Tarascan sculpture, carved mostly in volcanic stone; for example the great Chac-Mool of Ihuatzio, which shows Toltec influence; a throne or bench in the shape of a coyote; a human couple, seated; and what appears to be a

Ill. 146

dancing coyote.

Over a period of close on 300 years the Tarascans, like the Mexica, succeeded in consolidating a vast empire and imposing their language and customs on various peoples; but the Spanish Conquest brought their hegemony to an end, though their descendants still live on in Michoacán.

131 *(right)* Model of house with figures on a platform. Clay. Nayarit. Height: 31 cm. Classic

132 Hollow figures in black and red on cream. Clay. Chupícuaro, Guanajuato. Height: 17 cm. Upper Preclassic

134 Figurine with head partially shaven. Clay. El Opeño, Michoacán. Height: 12 cm. Middle Preclassic

133 Two musicians,
one whistling, the other
playing a drum. Clay.
Colima. Height: 13 cm.
Classic

135 Hollow seated
figure. Clay. Colima.
Height: 31 cm. Classic

136 *(left)* Vessel in the form of a reclining dog. Clay. Colima. Height: 14 cm. Classic

137 *(far left)* Hunch-backed old man with cane staff, standing on a two-headed fish. Clay. Jalisco. Height: 42 cm. Classic

138 *(left)* Nude woman kneeling. She has thin arms and a disfigured face. Clay. Nayarit. Height: 71 cm. Classic

139 Woman seated on bench. She has a misshapen head. Clay. Nayarit. Height: 56 cm. Classic

140 Mask with human features in outline. Stone. Mezcala. Height: 18 cm. Classic

141 (right) Mask in the form of a parakeet's head. Clay. Sinaloa. Height: 15 cm. Postclassic

142 Woman with scarification on her shoulders. Clay. Jalisco. Height: 40 cm. Classic

143 (right) Schematic models of temples. Stone. Mezcala. Height: 12 and 15 cm. Classic

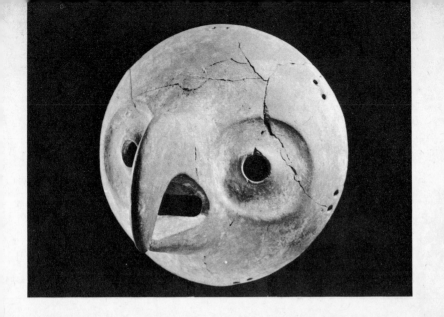

144 *(far left)* Vessel with stirrup handle and spout. Clay. Tzintzuntzan, Michoacán. Height: 22 cm. Postclassic. Tarasco

145 Mask of the god Xipe Totec. Copper. Tzintzuntzan, Michoacán. Height: 13 cm. Postclassic. Tarasco

146 *(far left, below)* Sculpture representing a coyote. Stone. Tzintzuntzan, Michoacán. Height: 53 cm. Postclassic. Tarasco

147 *(below)* Chac-Mool of Ihuatzio, Michoacán. Stone. Tarasco. Length: 1.57 m. Postclassic

THE ETHNOGRAPHICAL SECTION

Some four million indigenous people live an isolated existence in small villages and *rancherias* of Mexico, forming part of the rural population of the country. They still cultivate small plots of land planted with corn, chilli, beans, and squash, while weavers and potters pursue their crafts. The government is in the hands of elders or progressive young men; other aspects of their life are more closely linked to the past and to the supernatural.

As a result of the Spanish Conquest and colonization, the New World acquired swords and crosses, saints and machetes, along with sugar-cane, wheat, and the plough. Introduced at the same time were sheep and pigs, as well as baptism and the *compadrazgo* system (a fictitious kinship based on relationships between godparents and godchildren). In many cases these cultural elements became fundamental components of indigenous life and have persisted down to the present day.

The ethnographical section of the Museum occupies the upper storey of the building. There are ten large halls, each varying in size and design according to the quantity and nature of the materials to be exhibited.

Even so, not all the indigenous peoples of Mexico are represented; in planning the Museum it was necessary to concentrate on the most representative groups of certain natural and cultural areas. The absence of a hall devoted to the modern Aztecs or Mexicans had, however, another reason; namely, that to present the ethnography of the most widespread element of the community, numbering almost a million people scattered throughout twelve States, would have been virtually impossible.

As will be evident from the descriptions that follow, two or more groups which are ethnically and linguistically related, or share the same region or even the same geographic environment, occupy each hall. The material on display takes the form of maps and photographs showing the physical types, geographic location and environment of the groups; brief descriptions of historical antecedents; and the indication of certain socio-economic factors which distinguish the aboriginal cultures. By accompanying these with a representative selection of their material possessions a clear picture of each ethnic or Indian group emerges.

Since last century the commercialization of agricultural crops, the provision of educational institutions, the construction of highways, and increased social interchange have been transforming the cultural patterns of the indigenous population, making them participate more and more in the life of the nation.

Today the Indians have come to accept a political, social, and ceremonial centre – the municipal capital – in which are located the church, one or more stores, the houses of the *mestizos*, a school, a market-place, their political and religious leaders' humble dwellings, and offices for public services.

The various aboriginal peoples have many physical features in common, such as the dark, yellowish colour of their skin; straight black hair; dark eyes with slanting eyelids; thick lips, wide noses, and strong white teeth. Yet they have their individual traits as well. For instance, the Seris and Yaquis in the North-west are tall and long-legged, the Maya and the peoples of Oaxaca are characterized by a broad head and short limbs, while the Nahuas and Otomis are of a short stature and have a well-developed torso.

Introductory Hall

This introductory hall provides an over-all picture of what is presented in more detail in the various halls devoted to the individual cultures of Mexico. With the aid of materials and brief written explanations, the similarities and differences between the numerous indigenous cultures of Mexico are brought out, and their habits and customs compared.

The visitor is first introduced to photographs showing the variety of physical types; at the same time maps, mural paintings, and recorded commentaries serve to locate the cultures geographically and to render cultural and linguistic identification more readily understandable.

He then passes on to ample show-cases displaying examples of textiles, clothing, dyes, and adornments currently in use, together with drawings which illustrate types of apparel worn at different times during the Colonial period and also since Independence.

Next he is shown a colourful series of museographic units – for example, a group of women spinning and weaving, models of various types of huts, houses, and ground plots, and a huge granary – all meticulously and skilfully reconstructed. Around these are grouped further show-cases containing tools used in agriculture and the crafts, besides clay vessels of every shape and colour. Cooking utensils, the food prepared with them, as well as items of furniture are to be seen either in the original or reproduced in photographs.

A reliable picture of aboriginal and Colonial traditions can be formed from an examination of these utensils and tools and the end-products that resulted from their use. They include belt looms, spindles, spindle whorls, and distaffs; ploughs, machetes, and *coas* (digging sticks); the *quechquemitl, huipiles* (blouses), wrap-around and plain skirts; the three-stone hearth, spoons, plates, bowls, and the *comal* or clay disk for baking the maize *tortillas*.

Customs and beliefs that have survived from prehispanic times are also exemplified: there are tableaux showing distinctively attired persons engaged in magical, religious, and political activities. A display of feathers, votive disks, necklaces, sacred arrows, crosses and other objects, staffs of office, and various musical instruments enable the visitor to appreciate how certain human beliefs endured, while others underwent a transformation or fused. To fill in the background, there are numerous sketches and photographs.

Celebrations in honour of Catholic saints and festivities which have been held since Pre-Columbian times in memory of deceased relatives also receive attention. The extent to which the material has in the course of time impinged on the spiritual in the life of the people is shown in a group of exhibits that include gowns, embroidered capes, incense, candles, crosses, pictures, and a variety of offerings – in particular *panes de muertos* (bread baked in a special form and eaten on the Day of the Dead). Here again, photographs taken on the spot add to the authenticity of the ethnographic exhibits.

The Cora and Huichol Indians

Near the border between the States of Jalisco and Nayarit live some 15,000 descendants of the ancient Cora and Huichol Indians. The wild and inhospitable character of this region has allowed thousands of them to continue with their ancestral customs. Of the two groups, it is the Huichols who have retained the more prehispanic practices, particularly those connected with magic and religion which are surrounded by much secrecy.

While both groups devote themselves to agriculture, producing maize for sustenance, the Coras also have grazing lands for cattle and wool-producing animals, and grow fruit trees as well as agave or century plants for making textiles and preparing *mezcal*; this provides them with a cash income. Thereby the Coras have more contact with *mestizos*, can engage in itinerant commerce, and their integration into the rural life of the nation has been facilitated. By contrast, the Huichols are more isolated geographically and socially, their contacts with *mestizos* are rare, and so form a closed type of community. The habitat, geographic location, types of settlement, and territorial organization of both groups are illustrated by means of photographs and coloured maps.

For the most part the small Cora and Huichol communities have settled on the plains but a few occupy the valleys; their places of worship are still up in the mountains, where are to be found caves dedicated in particular to the cult of natural phenomena, animals, their bows and arrows and votive disks – primary symbols of their magico-religious cults.

The most usual type of dwelling is a hut with walls of clay and *zacate* roof, though among the Coras a rectangular house with stone or adobe walls is also quite common. Among the Huichols the kitchen and the granary for storing maize stand apart from the house, as can be seen from full-sized replicas in the hall.

A feature of Huichol clothing is its gorgeous colouring. The women wear wrap-around skirts and cotton shirts profusely embroidered with yarn of various colours; their woollen skirts are also embroidered, while ear-rings and necklaces made of small beads serve as ornaments. The men wear white cotton shirts and loose trousers, also embroidered with red and blue yarn; the indispensable *morral* (a bag worn over the shoulder) may be of wool or cotton but it is always embroidered with frets or stylized figures of animals. A straw hat with adornments of *Ill. 156* feathers and coloured ribbons completes the masculine attire. The dress of the *curanderos* (native doctors) is similar, except that they sport a large number of feathers and ribbons on their hats. Huichol garments of various kinds and a great number of their adornments can be seen both as exhibits in the show-cases and in the apparel worn by the life-size model figures.

Ill. 153 Some Huichol families live near the pagan oratory (*riquiri*) or in larger settlements containing the ceremonial centre (*calhiwey*). Their social and political organization is intimately bound up with their magico-religious cults and practices. The *curanderos* – soothsayers, and profoundly mystic individuals – are responsible for electing new political authorities, after entering a state of trance induced by consuming abundant *peyote*, *mezcal*, and *sotol* (an intoxicating beverage). Their distinctly religious life revolves round the *calhiwey* and the Catholic church, and their comparison of the morning star (Venus) with Jesus Christ, and the Sun and Moon with certain Catholic images, is evidence of a high degree of syncretism. Besides, the Huichols regard almost all natural phenomena as sacred. Arrows, shields, disks, and gourd bowls are believed to possess great supernatural power, and act as intermediaries between men and gods. An impression of this magico-religious world of the Huichols is vividly conveyed by means of a specially constructed device, with sound installations providing a background of prayers, sacred songs, and litanies.

The ceremonies connected with the *peyote* are the most important of the Huichol rituals. This cactus – metaphorically 'flower' – is traditionally a deer which converted itself into a grain of maize. Since maize is the staple of their diet, the Huichol believe the *peyote* to be an indispensable factor in obtaining a good harvest.

Tarascan Hall

Michuaque – place of fishes – is the name the Aztecs gave to the territory inhabited by the Tarascans. This is an upland area in the extensive central zone of what is now the State of Michoacán and takes in mountains and valleys and lakes.

The mountainous part, where conifers prevail, is the most extensive; the lake region occupies the centre of the plateau and includes Lake Patzcuaro and its picturesque islands. The geography and topography of these regions and the various types of settlements to be found there are illustrated by means of maps, charts, and large-scale photographs.

The indigenous population totals some 60,000 inhabitants most of whom are bilingual, speaking Tarascan and Spanish. There are variations in the physical appearance of the inhabitants, and these too are brought out in a series of photographs.

The precise origin of this group is not certain, but we know that in prehispanic times the Tarascans controlled a powerful dominion upon which the Aztecs repeatedly waged war, without being able to subjugate them.

Don Vasco de Quiroga, first Bishop of Patzcuaro, was a dominant force in the life of the Tarascans; he organized the towns around the 'hospitals' – institutions which in addition to attending the sick functioned as centres of various communal activities. Don Vasco in fact encouraged existing crafts and introduced new ones in his efforts to supply the natives with greater social and economic facilities. Brief explanatory labels describe the extra-ordinary course of colonial history in this part of Mexico.

At the present time agriculture is the most important economic activity of the Tarascans but even though those who live by or near the lakes also engage in fishing, they are not self-supporting. They therefore make articles for sale, which *cf. Ill. 150* include lacquer ware from Quiroga, guitars from Paracho, ceramics from Eronguarícuaro, copper objects from Santa Clara, wooden utensils from Pichátaro, and leather articles from Chilchotla, as well as producing straw hats, woollen *sarapes*, *rebozos*, fishing-nets, roof tiles, etc. There are numerous family workshops and some have installations that require master craftsmen, trained workmen, and apprentices. Almost all these crafts are exemplified in the hall, a wonderful piece of *Ill. 151* feather-work, an art no longer practised, being among the more fascinating exhibits.

Tarascans living in the highlands also take advantage of the resources of the forest. The picturesque *troje* – as their mountain dwellings are called – is made entirely of wood from its foundations up to the roof; it has a porch with artistically carved lintels and columns which serves as an antechamber to the main room. A full-size *troje* is on display. Elsewhere in the Tarascan zone the houses are built of stone or adobe with tile roofs.

The social and political organization of the Tarascans had their origin in forms introduced by the religious Orders in the sixteenth century. Thus in many mountain towns the traditional *guatapera* or centre for directing and planning communal works still operate. Here the legal and traditional authorities together with the principal people of the town assemble to discuss problems and their possible solutions, social gatherings and festivities take place, and justice is administered. More recently this institution has been fortified by the *Comisarios Ejidales* (delegates of collectively owned lands) and the Municipal Agencies.

Tarascan religious observance and practice are characterized by a merging of Christian ritual and native cult.

Ill. 149

On the Island of Janitzio for instance a mixture of Catholic and pagan rites is evident in the ceremonies commemorating the dead. The dance of the *Viejitos* (Old Men) and of the *Pescadores* (Fishermen), no less than accompanying music, express in tangible form the physical and socio-economic world of the Tarascans.

Otomi Hall

Legends and myths of prehispanic Mexico refer to the Otomis as hunters and gatherers. The Nahuatl word *otomitl* means foreign or nomadic; but it has been established linguistically that various groups who spoke – and still speak – Otomangue languages, which are interrelated, must have led a sedentary existence since ancient times.

Approximately 160,000 Otomis inhabit the plateaux and mountain ranges in the State of Hidalgo; 5,000 Chichimec-Jonaz and Pames the mountainous regions of San Luis Potosí and Guanajuato; some 70,000 Mazahuas and 30,000 Otomis are in the valleys and highlands of the State of Mexico, and about 10,000 others in Querétaro. Those of the Sierra Norte de Puebla are represented in another hall. These habitats of the principal Otomangue groups are shown in a series of photographs.

The first museographic unit is a tableau demonstrating the remarkable – almost dramatic – way in which the Otomis of the Valley of the Mezquital adapted themselves to a harsh environment. Here cultivation is limited owing to the pronounced aridity of the soil; consequently the *maguey* plant is exhaustively exploited. Its juice is used as *agua miel* ('sweet water') and *pulque*, parts of the pulpy leaves and stalk, as food; the leaves are used in the construction of huts and as fuel, and the fibres (*ixtle*) spun to produce many and varied kinds of yarns and fabrics.

In further illustration of this, there are show-cases containing tools used in the manufacture of *ayates* or bags, blankets, blouses, twine and rope, together with examples of these products, in all their various forms, finishes, and colours. Tools used in the production of woollen fabrics (*sarapes*, shirts, sashes, etc.), pottery jars, pitchers, and other vessels, as well as wicker baskets and other objects woven of reeds, are also on view, together with photographs of craftsmen at work and men and women engaged in domestic activities.

The Pames of San Luis Potosí are represented only by their coarse pottery and simple furniture, some wooden objects and implements. This ethnic group is in the process of losing its distinctive cultural characteristics.

The next section of the hall introduces the Mazahuas, who inhabit valleys and mountains of Ixtlahuaca and Atlacomulco. The visitor first sees a replica of one of their family adoratories, or shrines. These are generally erected amid the cultivated fields and are favoured sites for religious worship. Models of women wearing such garments as skirts made of coarse cotton muslin or taffeta, wrap-around skirts of woven wool, poplin blouses, and

Ill. 154 exquisite woollen *quechquemitl* illustrate the clothing of the Mazahuas and Otomis of these zones. Other figures are shown spinning and weaving. In addition, there are show-cases on the walls containing many colourful *quechquemitl*, woollen sashes or belts, musical instruments, tools, and examples of Mazahua and Otomi ceramics (jars, pitchers, and basins).

To illustrate fishing, which the Mazahuas and Otomis engage in at certain times of the year in lagoons and ponds, a circular net made of *ixtle* and a long harpoon with sharp point, used to catch *charales* (small lake fish) and trout respectively, are on view.

The closing section of the hall is devoted to the Otomis living in the mountains of Querétaro. Shown here, among other items, are beautiful *quechquemitl*; unfortunately these are going out of use since this ethnic-linguistic group is rapidly becoming integrated into the national culture.

The Northern Sierra of Puebla

Scattered over some fifty municipalities in the region known as the Sierra Norte de Puebla live about 150,000 indigenes who speak four different languages: Nahuatl (and a dialect of this known as Nahuat), Totonac, Otomi, and Tepehua.

Nahuas (some 70,000) and Totonacs (40,000) make up most of this total. Since up to three of the above-mentioned linguistic groups are to be found in any one municipality, there is a certain degree of cultural homogeneity in the region as a whole. Much of the zone used to be part of the ancient Totonacapan kingdom which after its disintegration was invaded by the Mexica, conquerors from the Central Highlands.

There is a concentration of the indigenous population in a region of the Sierra Madre Oriental. High up in these mountains the group of Nahuatl origin predominates; these people maintain themselves mainly by cultivating maize, and working on the land; they also make a certain amount of pottery, grow some fruit – peaches, apples, pears – and raise sheep, using the wool to make clothing.

Most of the Indians live in subtropical zones at altitudes roughly between 300 and 1,400 metres above sea-level. Frequent rains and a high degree of humidity keep the countryside green most of the year round, enabling them to grow two annual crops of maize, beans, and squash, and to produce and sell coffee, sugar-cane, and peanuts as well as tropical fruits.

The four ethnic groups have many cultural traits in common. All build huts with tree-trunks and mud, using *zacate* or clay tiles for roofing, and houses made of stone and tile; they store crops in *tapancos* (lofts) and small granaries, and use the *temazcal*

(steam bath of prehispanic origin) for hygienic, ritual, and therapeutic purposes. The women wear costume and adorn-
Ill. 157
Ill. 155
ments of non-Western origin, such as *enredos* (wrap-around skirts), *quechquemitl*, sashes, embroidered shirts, and *tochomites* (multicoloured cords for braiding into the hair) made on belt looms; the men, *ponchos* and loose white trousers of coarse unbleached cotton. In the fields the *coa* or digging stick is used. The way of life of these peoples receives ample coverage, either in the form of actual objects, or by means of photographs.

The four groups also have many customs in common, such as the manufacture of bark paper (*amate*) for ritualistic purposes and witchcraft (particularly distinctive of the Otomis); the employment of *topiles* (superintendents responsible for en-forcing communal labour); the retention of the *mayordomía* for organizing religious duties, and the use of shamanistic tech-niques both to effect cures and to inflict harm (witchcraft).

One of the more esoteric beliefs they share concerns a soul or double – shadow, *tona,* spirit – as well as the ability of a person to convert himself into a nocturnal bird and feed on human blood. They also believe in 'airs' or 'winds' being owners of hills or having the power to cause injury to the living, so that they must be placated with offerings placed on hills, in caves, and ravines; and in many other manifestations pertaining to both prehispanic and European folk-lore, including the Dances of the Flyers (Pole Dance), Quetzal Birds, and Bull Fighters.

Oaxaca Hall

Oaxaca is characterized by a number of social and cultural traits peculiar to the inhabitants of this region. For geographical and linguistic reasons, this large hall is divided into three main 'cultural areas': those of the Zapotecs and Huaves; of the Northern groups (Chinantecs and Mazatecs); and of the Mixtec region. These can, in turn, be subdivided.

At the present time Oaxaca contains some 800,000 in-habitants who speak native languages. The Mixtec element is

the largest, with nearly 300,000; next comes the Zapotec, with
some 250,000; then Mazatec, with around 100,000; Chinantec *Ills. 161, 158*
and Mixe account for about 50,000 each; the balance being
made up by folk speaking other languages again.

Among the Indians of Oaxaca, when houses and huts are
being built, the help of neighbours and relatives is always
expected and received. These huts are sparsely furnished.
Rustic wooden benches, nets of *ixtle* for storing things, palm
fibre *tenates* and other baskets, *cantaros* (water-jars) in various
shapes and sizes, *tapextles* and *petates* (woven reed mats) for
sleeping make up the household furnishings; in addition there
are stone *metates* for grinding, stone bowls, clay griddles and
jars; and *jicaras* and *calabazos* (gourd bowls).

The men are for the most part agriculturists, maize being the
principal crop and staple of their diet. However, some of the
Indians – when better lands become available, or through the
influence of the *mestizo* population and other nationals – plant
sugar-cane and wheat, which they sell. Coffee plantations are
common in the Zapotec mountainous regions, among the
Mazatecs, and in parts of the Chinantla, where tobacco and
rice are also cultivated. In the small valleys wheat is grown;
during much of the Colonial period these zones were regarded
as the grain-producing region of Oaxaca. Large quantities of
chilli peppers are cultivated in the Sierra Zapoteca del Norte
and in the Mixteca Baja, while in Tehuantepec the economy is
supported by fishing, the growing of cacao, and cattle-raising, *Ill. 165*
including a certain amount of trading in home-produced crops
and goods.

With reference to commerce, the Zapotecs use a system based
on territorial zones for their *tianguis* or markets. This allows for
a constant interchange of agricultural products and of local
and regional manufactured articles, besides offering opportuni-
ties for closer social relations and various forms of recreation.

The skill of the ancient inhabitants of Oaxaca in making
spectacular head-dresses and garments has been inherited by *Ill. 148*
their present-day descendants. Deserving of our admiration

185

cf. Ill. 152 are the unique dresses of the Yalalag and Tehuantepec women, and the brilliantly coloured embroidered sashes and blouses from Jalieza and San Antonino. That the Zapotecs have a well-developed aesthetic sense is attested by the handsome *sarapes* and woollen blankets made by the men of Teotitlán del Valle, which find a ready market. Where clay crafts are concerned, the vitreous ceramics of Atzompa and the grey and black pottery of Coyotepec are internationally famous. Examples of all these local products, and many more besides, are on display.

The indigenous families of Oaxaca now recognize both matrilineal and patrilineal descent, though the latter has priority. It is customary for a girl to live near the house of her in-laws, and the young husband must also render certain services to close relatives of his wife and reside with them for some months. Asking for a girl's hand in marriage is a very serious matter and 'petitioners' (*Huehuetlacas* or *Chigoles*) take charge of this. Marriages between blood relatives, and between those 'spiritually' related (godparents and godchildren) alone are proscribed. The *guelaguetza*, or system of reciprocal aid in money or in kind, is a well-established institution among the Zapotecs and provides whatever is needed for the celebration of marriages, wakes, and *mayordomías*.

The criterion in choosing a child's godparents is that they must be respectable people, whether or not they are relatives. So great is the mutual respect in which the relationship between the child's parents and these adopted relatives (the godparents) is held, that in the Chinantec region for example they perform a special ceremony known as 'washing the hands of the compadre'. In some regions children are provided with eight or ten god-parents, and conversely there are seniors – usually men – with fifty or sixty godchildren.

Members of religious and political institutions regularly perform public and private ceremonies and rites in which music, dances, and disguises are virtually indispensable. Special importance is attached to such events as taking office, *Cambio de Varas* (Change of Staff of Office) or *Aseguramiento de las*

Autoridades (Confirming the Authorities); to annual festivals in honour of patron saints' and other images of the Catholic Church, as well as to the performance of pagan rites, particularly in agriculture. They all make for solidarity and enhance the individual Indian's sense of belonging to his group and maintaining his cultural tradition.

The Gulf Coast Cultures

The three groups represented in this hall – Huastecs, Nahuas, and Totonacs – have inhabited the area of the Gulf Coast of Mexico since Pre-Columbian times. The Huastecs have bequeathed us numerous sculptures portraying gods and persons of importance, the Totonacs their representative yokes and *palmas* – not to mention the magnificent and strange pyramid of El Tajín.

It is estimated that currently some 90,000 people speak the Totonac language, including groups in the Sierra de Puebla. This hall is devoted to the culture of the inhabitants of El Tajín and Papantla.

Their economy is based mainly on the cultivation of vanilla, sugar-cane, maize, and a small quantity of fruit trees. They also engage in fishing, although on a small scale; among the fishing tackle shown are two different types of nets made by these people: a casting net and a 'spoon' or dipper-type net. This has been in use a very long time, for pictures of it appear in the ancient codices.

Totonac women excel at making certain textiles. They know how to spin cotton, which they use to weave cloth napkins on the ancient belt loom. The clothing on view shows the most characteristic garments of the women: the gauze *quechquemitl*, and a skirt embroidered in cross-stitch with brilliantly coloured thread.

Totonac dwellings are made of local materials. The huts are usually rectangular in shape with floors of tamped earth and with planks or bamboo for walls. There is always an altar with saints, candles, and flowers; on the Day of the Dead this altar is replete with offerings (*tamales*, brandy, clothing, etc.) for the souls who come to visit their kindred. All these aspects are covered by the exhibits, as are other important features of present-day Totonac culture such as music and the dance. In El Tajín and Papantla they perform dances known as 'Moors and Christians', 'Negritos', 'Santiagueros', and the 'Dance of the Flyers' or 'Pole Dance'; the last-named originates from an ancient solar cult.

Ill. 162 Some characteristics of the Nahua and Huastec cultures are treated in the second section of the hall. Here for example are to be found objects made from the *zapupe*, an agave plant from whose pulpy leaves a fine fibre is extracted for making *morrales* (shoulder bags), belts, and rope, a craft which the Huastecs of Veracruz have been practising for centuries.

Ill. 159 Their pottery, for the making of which very primitive techniques have been retained, is also represented. In Chililico, a town of Nahua-speakers tucked away in the mountainous
Ill. 160 Huastec district of Veracruz, a very individual type of pottery is produced, modelled by hand, painted a light colour, and decorated with floral motifs in brown.

The Huastecs make use of a variety of musical instruments of European and Pre-Columbian origin. There are examples here of harps, guitars, and violins to illustrate the former; the latter include small drums, rattles, reed flutes, and a *teponaxtle* (a horizontal wooden drum with two longitudinal tongues cut into the sounding-board).

Both in their dances and in their dress the Huastecs are traditionalists. The women wear beautiful clothing consisting of a wrap-around skirt tied to the waist and a *quechquemitl* with coloured embroidery; they complete their attire with a strange coiffure, formed by interweaving thick strands of yarn with their hair, which they wear like a head-dress.

The final exhibit in this hall is a small altar with flowers and food, representing part of a Huastec ceremony performed in
Ill. 163 thanksgiving for the new maize.

The Maya Halls

One of the largest indigenous groups of the American continent is that made up of peoples speaking the Maya language. All of them in one way or another are descendants of the creators of the extraordinary Maya civilization.

As in the prehispanic period, the Maya of today inhabit two large natural regions: the Lowlands and the Highlands. Occupying the Lowland region are approximately 30,000 Chontals of Tabasco, 200 to 300 Lacandon Indians, 40,000 Chols of Chiapas, and some 400,000 Maya of Yucatán, Campeche, and Quintana Roo; in the Highlands of Chiapas 100,000 Tzotzils, 60,000 Tzeltals, 30,000 Mames, and 15,000 Tojolabals, in round numbers, constitute the largest elements.

Each of these two main regions has a hall devoted to it, where photographs and mural paintings, show-cases, dioramas and tableaux serve to illustrate the more significant cultural features of its Maya inhabitants. Exhibited are their characteristic dwellings, their clothing, and their tools, as well as important aspects of their religious cult and magical practices. In addition, brief labels provide historical, demographic, social, economic, and political facts.

The initial unit shows something of the Chontals, and includes one of their characteristic huts made of wooden poles covered by a thatched roof, with its sparse furnishings and few domestic utensils. There are examples of ceremonial masks, and a typical fishing site is illustrated by means of photographs.

The visitor is next introduced to the Lacandon Indians, who are probably the most primitive element in Mexico. Tribally organized and peripheral to national life, they live in the tropical forests and woods, constantly moving their simple huts and strips of cultivation from one site to another. Two life-size models wearing dresses made of *majagua* bark and robes of coarse unbleached muslin show how they clothe themselves. *Ill. 167* Their agricultural activities are more or less confined to the growing of corn and tobacco, and these products, as well as domestic utensils, farming equipment, bows, arrows, and musical instruments peculiar to the Lacandon Indians, are exhibited in a number of show-cases.

Part of the *balche* ceremony is reproduced as a separate display, accompanied by a recording of songs and prayers connected with the ritual. *Balche* is an intoxicating beverage believed to possess magical properties.

The coverage of the Chol culture, about which little is known either past or present, has had to be confined to a few exhibits, mostly items of clothing.

The visitor then passes on to the Maya of Yucatán and Campeche. Here he will find a full-sized replica of a typical house, made of stones and with thatched roof, containing numerous utensils, as well as *huipiles* in a variety of designs and colours.

Ill. 168 The model of a woman is shown weaving fibres of *henequen* or hemp; near by appears a specimen of the plant itself, accompanied by photographs of the now-mechanized operations used to process it and the end-products thereby obtained – bags, shoulder bags, threads, twine, cords, handkerchiefs, and slippers. There are also several unique pieces of gold jewellery.

A diorama presenting in detail a pagan ceremony in which the rain god, Cha-Chac, is invoked in order to ensure a good crop of maize reveals the anxiety manifest in much of Mayan life.

The next hall is concerned with the Maya of the Highlands of Chiapas. Tzotzils and Tzeltals are grouped together since their social and cultural forms fall into a general pattern common to the whole area. Apart from subtle local variations, articles made of clay and wood, headgear, clothing, and adornments are alike, so these form a composite exhibit, with an indication of the provenance of each item.

The *tianguis* are represented by a charming scene in which 16 *Ill. 170* figures dressed in a variety of present-day garments representing 16 different municipalities appear.

A model illustrating a Chamula ground plot provides a synthesis of the domestic life of this group. A group of nine appropriately attired figures serve to illustrate wedding apparel, as well as the clothing and disguises worn on special occasions such as the investiture of religious and political officials, Carnival festivities, and ceremonies in honour of Catholic saints.   *Ill. 171*

In conclusion there are exhibits relating to the cult of the cross, a mural painting which interprets the magic world of the Highland Maya, and a domestic altar used by Mames and Tojolabals. At present no ethnographic materials are available for these two last-mentioned groups, but a salvage programme has been instituted by the Museum, and this should provide new acquisitions to make up the deficiency.

North-western Mexico

Politically and geographically North-western Mexico comprises the Peninsula of Lower California, the State of Sonora, the central and western parts of Chihuahua, and northern Sinaloa. Desert, coastal plains, and mountains characterize this extensive region, and at the same time lend indigenous cultures an individual aspect.

Of the various groups inhabiting this area three – the Seris, Tarahumaras, and Yaquis – are represented in this hall. These peoples remained marginal to Mesoamerican civilization and lived mainly by hunting, gathering, and fishing, although the Yaquis later learned to practise agriculture and pottery. War and extermination characterized their first contacts with the white man, but Jesuit and Franciscan missions left an indelible impression on cultural forms which still persist.

The Seris, inhabiting two small localities in Sonora, constitute one of the smallest groups; they number scarcely 300. Some important aspects of their culture are a barter economy based on catching sea-turtles; basketwork similar to that of groups in   *Ill. 166* the United States Southwest; facial painting by the women; and ceremonies invoking magic such as puberty rites and ritual games with sticks. The most typical designs of facial painting are among the exhibits.

The Tarahumaras, numbering approximately 50,000, inhabit the region known as the Sierra Tarahumara. In the high valleys they practise slash-and-burn agriculture, put wood to a variety of uses, and make woollen garments. However, in the winter, when they move to the deep ravines, using natural caves as dwellings, they engage in crafts employing palm fibres and live on a modified diet that includes chilli, onions, and tomatoes.

Of particular importance where the ceremonial side of Tarahumaran life is concerned are native doctors who specialize in the *peyote* cult and ritual sacrifice of large cattle. These events are accompanied by songs and dances, some of Colonial origin and others prehispanic. These aspects are illustrated by means of colour photographs, supplemented by a variety of objects used on these occasions.

That leaves the Yaquis, who represent the coastal plains culture and number some 12,000 souls. They are congregated in eight towns scattered over an area of approximately 540,000 hectares, and their principal characteristic is the high regard they have for the land. They regard it as having been a divine gift, and their habits and customs are intelligible only within this context.

The social, political, and religious organization of the Yaquis derives from the framework established by the Jesuits during the period when these people were under tutelage.

Ill. 164   Music and the dance constitute another important aspect of their culture. The Deer Dance and that performed by the Pascolas are especially noteworthy, in that they are artistically conceived and dramatically rendered by singularly agile performers. Sculptures in natural size, as well as musical instruments, masks, and unusual adornments used on clothing occupy this last section of the hall devoted to the Yaquis.

Modern Autochthonous Mexico

The last hall of the Ethnographical Section presents a synthesis of the process of social and cultural change taking place in Mexico today. On view at the entrance is a photographic mosaic illustrating various projects (economic, educational, health, etc.) calling for the participation of the native peoples, through which the National Indigenist Institute is trying to integrate the various ethnic groups into Mexican national life.

Facing this mosaic is another unit which expresses in a clear and dignified manner the juridical and philosophic principle of Benito Juarez, who as President of the Mexican Republic set the country on the road to progress: Respect for the rights of others signifies peace.

By means of photographs, paintings, and products of native crafts, the next section of the hall shows changes that have occurred in Mexican culture and society through the centuries: prehispanic ceremonial centres, the ancient Cathedral of Mexico City from Colonial days, as well as the superb architecture of the present National University of Mexico. In addition, there are reproductions of prehispanic paintings pertaining to food, music, the dance, and feats of war; and these are offset by photographs of today's National Symphonic Orchestra and Modern Ballet, together with paintings by contemporary artists, notably Diego Rivera.

Next, works of prehispanic poets are contrasted with excerpts from the writings of outstanding present-day Mexican poets. To conclude, a cross-section of the popular crafts of Mexico is presented in the shape of objects made of ceramic, copper, tin, palm fibre, and wood.

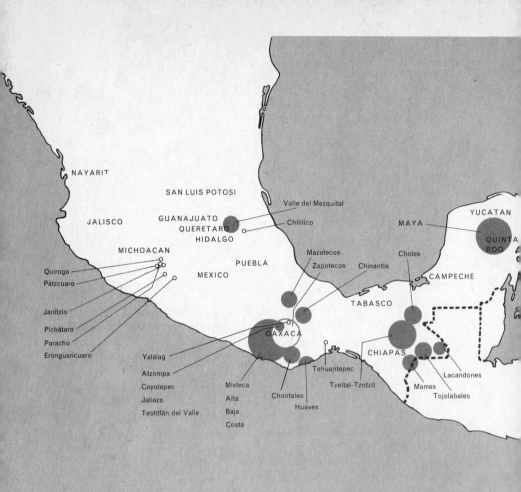

NAYARIT

SAN LUIS POTOSI

Valle del Mezquital

JALISCO

GUANAJUATO
QUERETARO
HIDALGO

Chililico

MICHOACAN

PUEBLA

MAYA

YUCATAN

QUINTA
ROO

Quiroga
Pátzcuaro

MEXICO

Mazatecos
Zapotecos

Chinantla

Choles

CAMPECHE

Janitzio

Pichátaro

Paracho

Eronguaricuaro

OAXACA

TABASCO

CHIAPAS

Lacandones

Yalalag

Atzompa

Coyotepec

Jalieza

Teotitlán del Valle

Mixteca

Alta

Baja

Costa

Chontales

Huaves

Tehuantepec

Tzeltal-Tzotzil

Mames

Tojolabales

Main cultural areas of Mexico

194

148 Costume worn by dancers in the famous Feather Dance, performed regularly by the Zapotecs of the Valley of Oaxaca.

149 Wooden mask used for certain festivals by the Tarascans

151 (right) Small altarpiece made of feathers, showing a Catholic Virgin. Example of ancient craft practised by Tarascans

150 Pieces of early lacquer ware from Uruapan, Michoacán

152 Four costumes from Oaxaca: from left to right as used by the Triqui from Copala, the Zapotecs from the Isthmus (ancient costumes), the Mixe from Cotzocón and the Cinantecs of Ojitlán

153 Domestic shrine of the Huichols

154 *Quechquemitl* and bag used by the Otomi peoples. They are of prehispanic origin

155 *(far right)* Hand-embroidered blouse, used by Nahua women of Tla-comulco, Sierra de Puebla

156 Clothing worn by Huichol shaman

157 *(right)* Costume worn by Nahua women from the Sierra de Puebla

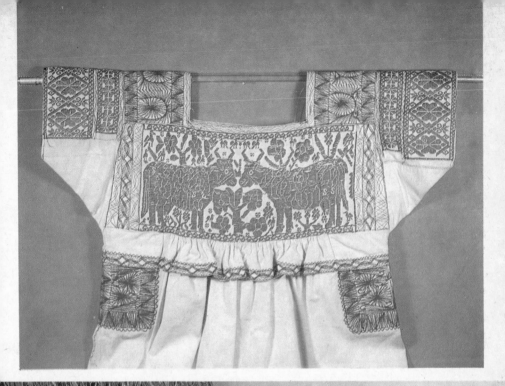

158 *(above, left)* Vessels from the Mixtec region of Acatlán, Puebla

159 *(above)* Huastec vessel from Tantobal, Valles, San Luis Potosí

160 Nahua potters of Chililico, Huejutla, Hidalgo. The type of ware made by them is in common use in the Huastec region

161 Chinantec woman (standing) and a Mazatec woman from Jalapa de Díaz carding cotton to prepare it for spinning

162 (*right*) Woman weaving *zapupe* fibre, Tantoyuca, Veracruz

163 (*right, below*) Scene from the Huastec Ceremony for the New Maize

CEREMONIA DEL MAIZ NUEVO

164 Stag and human masks. The Deer Dance and the *Pascola* are the most representative dances of the Yaquis and Mayos of Sonora

167 Lacandon woman with items of domestic equipment: loom, gourd bowls, low bench for making tortillas, coarse clay vessel and shoulder-bag containing various clay vessels and gourd bowls

166 Seri baskets, called *coritas,* woven with spiral bands, are quite similar to those made in the United States Southwest

165 Net, basket and three-pronged harpoon used for fishing in rivers and streams of the Chinantec region in Oaxaca

168 Maya woman of Yucatán wearing a *huipil*, weaving *henequen* fibre to manufacture *morrales* (shoulder-bags)

169 *(left)* Popular clay crafts: the 'arbol de la vida' (tree of life) and the mermaid from Metepec, State of Mexico; vessels from Tzintzuntzan and Patamban (Michoacán) and copper articles from Santa Clara, Michoacán

170 *(left, below)* Scene showing the different styles of Indian costume that distinguish the inhabitants of the Chiapas Highlands

171 Pair of *mayordomos,* who supervise the veneration of Catholic images, wearing clothing characteristic of Tenejapa in the Chiapas Highlands

Glossary

Including Nahua and Spanish terms used in Text

Acamapichtli — First Mexica ruler, AD 1376–96

'Acatlaxqui' — Dance performed in some Nahua and Otomí towns in the region of Pahuatlán, Puebla.

Aguamiel — Juice from the heart of the century plant (*Agave americana*), a member of the Amaryllis family, from which *pulque* (*q.v.*) is made.

Ah Puch — Maya god of death, lord of darkness and of drought.

Ahuizotl — Eighth ruler of Tenochtitlán, AD 1486–1502.

Alcalde — Indian civil functionary in the older traditional town government, which has been supplanted by the municipal government.

Atarraya — Round, easily cast net with weights, used for fishing.

Atlatl — Dart- or spear-thrower.

Axayacatl — Sixth ruler of Tenochtitlán, AD 1469–81.

Bacabes, or Bacabs — Among the Maya, beings stationed in the four directions or cardinal points who supported the world. They were also year-bearers.

Baktún — Period of 144,000 days, used in the Maya Long Count.

Balche — A fermented beverage prepared by the Maya by soaking skins of various fruits with bark of the Lonchocarpus tree and honey.

Cabecera — Town in which the government of a *municipio* (*q.v.*) is established.

Calmecac — 'Row of houses.' School where sons of noblemen were educated.

Chac — Among the Maya, the god of rain and related phenomena, such as thunder, lightning, etc. He had four assistants called Chaques.

Chac-Mool — Sculpture of a reclining individual with a receptacle upon his stomach for hearts of sacrificial victims.

Chalchiuhtlicue — 'She of the jade skirt', goddess of the waters, companion of Tlaloc.

Chicomecoatl — '7 serpent', Aztec earth goddess.

Chimalpopoca — Third ruler of Tenochtitlán, AD 1417–27.

Charola (batea de madera) — Receptacle of circular or quadrangular shape carved from a single piece of wood and usually wider at the mouth than at the base.

Coatepantli — Wall of serpents.

Coatlicue — 'She of the serpent skirt', goddess of the earth, mother of the gods.

Cocijo — 'Lightning', Zapotec god of rain.

Codex — Book in the form of a folding screen, made of deerskin or bark paper, and painted with hieroglyphs and figures.

Comisariado ejidal — Group of authorities in charge of administering and directing agricultural work and enforcing agrarian laws on the *ejido* (*q.v.*).

Copal — Aromatic resin used as incense in religious ceremonies.

Coyolxauhqui — Lunar goddess; sister of Huitzilopochtli – the sun.

Cuauhtemoc — 'Eagle who fell.' Last ruler of the Mexica who tenaciously defended Tenochtitlán against the Spaniards (AD 1521).

Cuauhxicalli — Vase or container for holding human sacrificial offerings.

Cueraváperi — Creator goddess, mother of the deities; feminine principle in the creation.

Cuitlahuac — Tenth ruler of Tenochtitlán, AD 1520.

Curicaveri — The most important god of the Tarascans; the sun and fire and all that related to these elements.

Eccentric axes — Objects carved of flint or obsidian in whimsical forms, including human figures in silhouette. They were common in the Maya region.

Ehecatl — Mexica god of wind. He is represented wearing a duck-billed buccal mask.

Ejido — Collectively-owned agricultural and pasture lands of a village, recognized by law.

Encomendero — In Colonial times a Spaniard to whom Indian settlements were entrusted.

Grooved axe — Stone implement of petaloid shape with a groove for tying or fastening it to a handle. The groove may encircle the entire axe or only three-quarters of it.

'Guaguas' — Dance in which a cross made of four poles is erected high in the air on which four men climb to make it revolve. Of ancient origin, this dance is performed in the region of Pahuatlán, Puebla, and Papantla, Veracruz.

Huehueteotl	'Old God.' Deity of fire and god of the centre of the earth.
Huipil	A long sleeveless shirt frequently worn by the prehispanic Maya.
Huitzilihuitl	Second Mexica ruler, son of Acamapichtli, AD 1396–1417.
Huitzilopochtli	'Hummingbird of the south.' God of war who occupied the seventh heaven; his colour was blue.
Hunab Kú	Supreme god of the Maya. Creator of all existing things.
Ik	Maya god of wind and one of the days of the calendar. He had four helpers called Iques.
Itzamná	'Dew from Heaven.' Maya god related to celestial phenomena.
Itzcoatl	Fourth ruler of Tenochtitlán, AD 1427–40. Famous reformer of the Mexica Empire.
Jícara	Bowl made from a gourd.
Katún	Period of 7200 days, used in the Maya Long Count.
Kín	Unit of time (a day), used in the Maya Long Count. Sun or lord.
Kukulkán	Bird-serpent. Deified culture hero, equivalent of the Mexica Quetzalcoatl (*q.v.*).
Labret	Ornament which was inserted in the lower lip. It was usually cylindrical and had lateral wings.
Macuilxóchitl	'Five Flower.' God of games and recreation. He was usually shown emerging from a turtle carapace.
Majagua	Carib word designating a tree of the Malvacean family. The timber obtained from it is very hard.
Matachines	Dance of Colonial origin adopted by the Yaqui, Mayo, and Tarahumara Indians.
Maxtlatl or Maxtle	Item of clothing similar to a loin-cloth.
Mayordomo	Church official who is custodian of the image of a saint or virgin and hence responsible for seeing that their cult is observed.
Mictlantecuhtli	Lord of the dead and of hell.
Mixcoatl	'Cloud Serpent.' The Milky Way and god of the hunt.
Moctezuma I	Fifth ruler of Tenochtitlán, AD 1440–69.
Moctezuma II	Ninth ruler of Tenochtitlán, AD 1502–20.
'Moros y Cristianos'	Dance re-enacting a battle between Catholic Spaniards and the infidels or Moors. Today this is the surviving form of a dance introduced a few years after the Conquest.
Municipo	The smallest administrative subdivision of the State.
Nawal	Term for witch-doctors in whom specific powers are vested.
'Negritos'	Dance performed by a group of men one of whom is dressed as a woman and represents Malinche (the Indian slave-girl who became mistress and willing helper of Cortes); others wear masks and play the role of buffoons.
Novena	A ritual recitation of Catholic prayers, in church or at home, on one night or on a series of nights.
Padrinos	The sponsors or god-parents of a child at baptism or marriage.
Palma	Sculpture carved in stone for funerary purposes. It is related to the ball-game and may represent a plastron worn by the players.
Patojo	Vessel shaped like a foot or shoe.
Patolli	Game similar to Royal Goose. It was played with beans or sticks marked with spots like dice, and on a reed mat painted with a cross-shaped design.
Peyote	A cactus rich in peyotine and mezcaline used by several Indian groups in magic ceremonies.
Pinole	A seasoned drink or gruel made of maize ground and toasted.
Pizarra Yucateca	Yucatecan slate ware. Pottery with soapy, lustrous appearance, made in the Yucatán Peninsula during the Puuc period, AD 600–1000.
Plumbate ware	Partially vitrified pottery, the surface of which has a metallic lustre.
Posole	An unfermented beverage of maize and water.
'Principales'	Group of highly respected persons who have acquired vast experience through services rendered to the town in administrative, political, and religious offices.
Promesa	A vow or sacred promise.
Pueblo	A legally recognized category of municipal settlement having a government organization which includes a commissary and other officials.
Pulque	Beverage with low alcoholic content prepared from fermented *aguamiel* (*q.v.*).
Quecholli	'Bird of rich plumage.' Month of the Mexica year dedicated to Mixcoatl, god of the hunt.
Quechquemitl	Shawl covering the breast and

211

Glossary

Quetzalcoatl 'Plumed Serpent.' Both a Nahua god and a culture hero. He is related to the planet Venus, the wind, and also has other aspects.

'Quetzales' Dance probably of prehispanic origin which is famous today among the Nahuat people of Cuetzalan, Puebla. Its distinctive feature is an enormous head-dress adorned with ribbons and feathers in brilliant colours.

Ranchería Small unincorporated settlement.

Rebozo Shawl covering the head and shoulders, traditionally worn by women.

Red de Cucharón Small circular net tied to a pole, for catching fish.

Regidor Elected town council official.

Rezadora Woman adept at reciting Catholic prayers who serves at novenas (*q.v.*) and other ceremonies.

'Santiagueros' Dance representing the struggle of the Spaniards against the Moors. The principal character rides a wooden horse and holds a sword in his hand.

Sarape Blanket worn as male attire.

Shaft-tomb Burial structure comprising a chimney or descent shaft and one or more intercommunicating rooms.

Stirrup-spout handle Handle formed by a curved hollow tube with a short neck or spout in the middle where liquid can be poured in or out.

Tamal A dish made from maize dough with a great many alternate flavourings, including chilli pepper sauce and sweetened cinnamon.

Tapextle Crude bed, consisting of a framework of wood, strengthened with rods or canes and supported on four forked sticks.

Tariácuri Tarascan god and culture hero, similar to the Mexican Quetzalcoatl (*q.v.*)

Tecomate Globular jar without neck or rim; the term also refers to a vessel shaped like a gourd-bowl.

Telar de cintura Belt or back-strap loom, one end of which is fastened to a post, the other tied to the weaver's waist.

Telpochcalli Popular school where boys were trained for war.

Temalacatl Circular stone where gladiatorial combat took place before sacrifice.

Teocalli 'House of god', temple.

Tepeyolohtli 'Heart of the mountain'. Jaguar.

Tequila Intoxicating liquor distilled from the roasted stems of the *Agave tequilana,* a type of century plant.

Thin Orange Teotihuacán pottery having very thin walls and an orange slip. It was used for commerce.

Tianguis Native market held every week on a certain day at established sites.

Tizoc Seventh ruler of Tenochtitlán and famous conqueror, AD 1481–86.

Tlachtemalacatl Ring of wood or stone used in the ball-game. If of stone, it was attached to the side wall of the court and the players had to try to pass the ball through it.

Tlachtli Field for the ball-game which had the form of a capital I.

Tlahuizcalpante-cuhtli 'Lord of the House of Dawn.' The planet Venus as Morning Star.

Tlaloc God of rain and lightning.

Tlalocan Paradise of Tlaloc, abode of those whose death was attributed to water (drowning, dropsy, etc.).

Tlazolteotl Goddess associated with fertility and birth. Mother of Centeotl, god of maize.

'Tocotines' Dance performed by Tepehua and Totonac men of the Puebla Mountains, wearing crowns and capes and carrying rattles. In certain towns the dance is presented by a group of girls who wear crowns of flowers and carry rattles.

Tonalpohualli Mexica religious calendar of 260 days.

Tonatiuh Solar god of the Mexica.

Topiles Young men employed by the *municipio* (*q.v.*). They are on the first rung of the ladder in the municipal government or in the religious structure. They are also called 'semaneros'.

ti'Toreadores' Dance simulating a bull-fight, with the animal represented by a dancer wearing a bull's head and a framework covered with the animal's skin. In the Puebla Mountains a drum and flute provide accompaniment.

Totonacapan In ancient times the land of the Totonacs, comprising part of the Gulf Coast and extending as far as the Puebla Mountains. Its main centre was Cempoala.

Tún Period of 360 days, almost a solar

	year, used in the Maya Long Count.
Uinal •	Period of 20 days, used in the Maya Long Count.
Voladores	Name for participants in the 'Pole Dance'.
Xipe Totec	'Our lord the flayed one.' God of spring-time and of jewellers.
Xiuhcoatl	The fire serpent. He accompanied the sun in its journey through the firmament.
Xiuhtecuhtli	Lord of the year, of grass, of turquoise, and of fire.
Xocotlhuetzi	Month of Aztec calendar in which the ceremony of the falling fruit was celebrated.
Xochipilli	Prince of flowers, patron of the dance, games and love.
Xochiquetzal	Goddess of love and beauty. Patroness of domestic work and of flowers.
Yácata	Temple base combining rectangular and circular elements, typical of Tarascan architecture.
Yerbatero, -a	Spanish term for a shaman, and more generally a person who treats illness with herbs.
Yoke	Sculpture carved in stone for funerary purposes in the form of a horseshoe and representing the wide protective belts worn by ball-players.

Museum Catalogue Numbers of Items Illustrated

4 4–1751	43 15–103	81 1–3331	121 5–1005
5 4–1776	44 15–199	82 13–456	122 5–113
6 13–784	45 11–3330	83 13–428	125 12–945
7 20–730	46 11–3225	84 13–419	126 12–617
8 1–2390	47 11–3224	85 4–1887	127 12–608, 12–614
9 1–3364	48 11–3425	86 4–1090	128 12–682
10 1–3363	49 11–3295	87 4–998	129 12–978
11 1–3365	50 11–3290	88 4–1831	130 12–537, 12–561
12 1–2298	51 11–2767	89 4–1002	131 2–4849
13 1–2578	52 11–3291	90 4–1889	132 2–4843, 2–4894
14 1–2342	53 11–2774	91 4–984	133 2–5616, 2–6148
15 1–2705, 1–2703	54 11–3729	92 4–988	134 2–1666
16 1–2472, 1–2469,	55 11–3015	93 4–1009	135 2–3465
1–2270, 1–2484	56 11–3426	94 4–1006	136 2–5447
17 1–557	57 11–2765	95, 96 3–588	137 2–1345
18 1–1321, 1–1322	58 11–2606	97 3–531	138 2–5866
19 9–2548	59 11–2916	98 4–1926	139 2–4932
20 9–2557	60 11–2759	99 3–402	140 2–4996
21 9–2859	61 6–4681	100 3–541	141 2–6123
22 9–2498	62 6–5311	101 3–391	142 2–4816
23 9–686	63 6–29	102 3–590	143 2–4992, 2–4993
24 9–2407	64 6–6071	103 5–75	144 2–6112
25 9–2566	65 6–6001	104 5–1210	145 2–4263
26 9–1697	66 7–1695, 7–1696	105 5–1411	146 2–6466
27 9–3283	67 6–4846	106 5–1037	147 2–6465
28 9–1700	68 6–6439	107 5–564	149 28377(63)20.29–492
29 9–500	69 6–55	108 5–1636	150 25455(63)20.156g–180,
30 9–759	70 7–2342	109 5–1763	25667(61)20.156g–388
31 9–2847	71 7–2345	110 5–1651	154 25108(61)14.38c–195,
32 14–10	72 7–2337	111 5–1644	24813(61)13.38c–38
33 14–9	73 7–2539	112 5–1637	155 64635(64)9.13g10–850
34 14–2	74 7–2687, 7–2685,	113 5–1676	158 28596(63)9.37a1–527,
35 15–62, 15–68, 15–65	7–2313	114 5–1761	28674(63)9.37a1–545
36 15–35	75 3–587	115 5–1473	159 67292(64)14.36a1–497
37 15–151	76 13–621	116 5–1762	164 26679(63)30.31f7c–64,
38, 39 15–196	77 13–659	117 5–1083	33308(63)30.31f7c–166
40 15–169	78 4–1007	118 5–1638	166 34869(64)30.0863–40,
41 15–104	79 13–533	119 5–1060	34872(64)30.08b3–43,
42 15–27	80 13–420	120 5–1764	34887(64)30.08b3–58

Index of Names

214